CATHOLIC REFORM

CATHOLIC REFORM

FROM CARDINAL XIMENES TO THE COUNCIL OF TRENT 1495–1563

AN ESSAY WITH
ILLUSTRATIVE DOCUMENTS AND
A BRIEF STUDY OF ST. IGNATIUS LOYOLA

JOHN C. OLIN

Fordham University Press
New York
1990

TO MY SON JOHN
πολλῶν οὕνεκα

CONTENTS

PREFACE

The sixteenth century in European history is marked by the religious upheaval we call the Reformation, and attention is generally focused on Luther and the other Protestant reformers who broke with the established Church and preached new doctrines and practices. But this development, major as it is, is not the whole story of reform in the sixteenth century. Underlying and encompassing it was a broader search for religious renewal and reform. In my introductory essay and its accompanying documents I shall look at other efforts, distinct from the Protestant ones, to achieve these goals. The efforts I shall discuss remained within the ambit of the existing Catholic Church and constitute a movement that is sometimes referred to as the Catholic Reformation.

This reform movement can be distinguished not only from the Protestant Reformation, which began with the famous indulgence controversy in 1517, but also from the Counter-Reformation, as it is called, which in the original meaning of the term refers to the militant Catholic reaction to the Protestant challenge. Catholic reform in a more positive sense had a different origin and purpose. It did not begin in opposition to Protestantism but was a parallel movement, so to speak, springing out of the same context and responding to very similar needs for religious change and revival. Its manifestations in fact antedate Luther's revolt. Its purpose was to correct ills in the Church and reinvigorate its life and mission. It was profoundly affected by the crisis and schism that developed after 1517, but it did not suddenly arise then. It was, however, given new urgency and a new dimension by the serious problems that were now posed, and a complex pattern of Catholic activity unfolded under the shock of widespread dissension and revolt. We cannot simply label it the Counter-Reformation. The term is too narrow and misleading. The survival of Catholicism as well as the lives of many of the most important Catholic figures of the time and the nature of many events demand another and a broader perspective. Renewal and reform continued within the framework of the Church's teaching and authority, though inevitably these efforts tended to merge with the defense of the institution and the struggle to maintain and restore it.

This study will focus, then, on reform efforts that remained within the Catholic fold. As the title indicates, I shall look at the scene from the time of Cardinal Ximenes to the Council of Trent, that is, from the years 1495 to 1563. Francisco Ximenes de Cisneros became archbishop of Toledo and primate in Spain in 1495 and undertook a significant work of religious reform. His initiatives afford a convenient and viable point of departure. The Council of Trent ended its sessions in 1563, and its achievements are a culmination in a sense of all that went before. They close an era and open a new and important one in the history of the Catholic Church. We have thus a period of almost seventy years to observe the phenomenon of Catholic reform, years of profound historical change and years of crucial importance for the survival and revival of the Catholic faith.

Let me note at the outset that the subject I am about to deal with is complex and fraught with a number of historiographical and interpretive problems. These latter concern differences of approach and focus, on the one hand, and of understanding and evaluation, on the other. The divergencies both in general outlook and on specific points that one encounters can be extremely confusing. I do not want to enter into a lengthy bibliographical discussion in this slender volume, but attention should be called to this matter if for no other reason than to indicate my own point of view and better situate the essay I have written. It breaks, for instance, with the conventional stereotype of Protestant Reformation and Catholic Counter-Reformation to view Catholic reform in a more positive and emphatic way, and its focus, as I have already stressed, will be on what is happening in the Catholic Church to revitalize its faith and life. This is a different approach from the one that is found in most Reformation studies and texts, which generally treat their subject from the vantage point of the Protestant revolt and give short shrift to the question of Catholic reform. Steven Ozment's *The Age of Reform, 1250–1550* (New Haven: Yale University Press, 1980), a substantial and probing work within the limits of its theme, is a fairly recent example of this. Ozment also, as his time span allows, links the Protestant revolt to divisive and heterodox currents in the later Middle Ages and to the failure of the late medieval Church to satisfy "aggrieved hearts and minds." The latter is a common thesis, though it does not go uncontested. The notion of "the unresponsiveness of the late medieval Church" has been seriously challenged in an article bearing that title by Lawrence G. Duggan in *The Sixteenth Century Journal* of April 1978 that actually reverses that standard point of view, and the companion theme of "accelerating decline" in the Church in the fourteenth and fifteenth centuries leading inevitably to the religious crisis and Protestantism in the sixteenth century has been rejected by Francis Oakley in his *The Western Church in the Later Middle Ages* (Ithaca: Cornell University Press, 1979).

It is not an easy task to ascertain the causal relationships and find the proper balance among the numerous currents and developments that confront us in this age. I am, however, concerned here less with an analysis of the historical scene as a whole than with a description of a single movement during the period I have defined or at least of major aspects of it. Nevertheless the larger context has to be borne in mind, and the limitations of this study have to be acknowledged. I am aware indeed that I am not offering a comprehensive treatment or a definitive evaluation of Catholic reform. Two recent studies have made me particularly conscious of that: John Bossy's *Christianity in the West, 1400–1700* (Oxford: Oxford University Press, 1985) and Barbara McClung Hallman's *Italian Cardinals, Reform, and the Church as Property* (Berkeley: University of California Press, 1985). They reveal other approaches to the subject and deal with facets of the story that I have not developed. Bossy's work is a descriptive survey of popular beliefs and practices before the Reformation and of changes wrought therein in the sixteenth century. It is a history not of events or of the Church as an institution but of religious attitudes and sensibilities. Hallman's work is quite different. It is a monographic study of the Italian cardinals in the period I am covering and of their wealth, holdings, and family relationships, and it documents the failure of reform with regard to some very serious abuses plaguing the Church in this era. Its conclusions are certainly important to ponder in passing judgment on the effectiveness of Catholic reform.

I want also to point out an assumption underlying this study: I assume that Catholic reform at this time is a coherent and constructive movement deserving close attention. It is an assumption that some historians may not readily accept and that some may feel is incongruous with a general interpretation they themselves profess. In this regard Robert Mandrou's *From Humanism to Science, 1480–1700* (Harmondsworth: Penguin, 1978) springs to mind. Mandrou views the changing times he surveys in terms of a clash between "new ideas" and a narrow orthodoxy maintained by the Church, that is, between everything innovative and Catholic tradition. Needless to say, a very different perspective informs the essay presented here. It will follow in general the approach and concur with the tenor of H. Outram Evennett's *The Spirit of the Counter-Reformation* (Cambridge: Cambridge University Press, 1968). That work, although unfortunately the term "Counter-Reformation" is used in its title, stresses the positive, even creative, side of Catholic reform in the sixteenth century and sees the movement as the process of inner renewal and outward adaptation that the post-medieval Church underwent. I am reminded in this connection of a passage in Henri de Lubac's *Catholicism* (New York: Longmans, 1950) wherein he remarks that the Church is in "a continual state of rebuilding" and has undergone many changes in style over the centuries. Reform, he states, must be not simply a return to the past but rather an assimilation of tradition and an adaptation to present needs and problems. *Aggiornamento* is a recent term that might be applied to this process.

In addition to the essay on Catholic reform, this volume contains several documents that supplement the narrative text and illustrate from contemporary sources the character of the movement I am examining. Appended also is a brief study of mine of St. Ignatius Loyola, which first appeared in *Church History*, the journal of the American Society of Church History, in December 1979. Ignatius is perhaps the most important person in our story, and this article, I hope, will further clarify his thought and mission. In composing and preparing this present volume I have drawn especially on two earlier publications of mine that have been out of print for some time. One is a collection of fifteen documents relating to reform in the Church in the period 1495 to 1540 entitled *The Catholic Reformation: Savonarola to Ignatius Loyola* and published by Harper & Row in New York in 1969. Two of the documents in the present volume have been taken from the earlier collection, viz., the address of Egidio da Viterbo at the Fifth Lateran Council and the *Consilium de emendanda ecclesia*. I shall refer frequently to this previous work, both to its documents and to the introductory notes and bibliography that accompany them. The other publication is a chapter I wrote entitled "The Catholic Reformation" for *The Meaning of the Renaissance and Reformation*, edited by Richard L. DeMolen and published by Houghton Mifflin in Boston in 1974. My present essay is a revision and amplification of that chapter. I am indebted, of course, to many other sources as well, as my notes and references here will indicate, though these are intended primarily to serve as guides to further reading and investigation. In conclusion I should like to mention a recent work, a chapter of which bears some resemblance at least in tone and point of view to this survey of mine: Eric Cochrane's posthumous *Italy, 1530–1630*, edited by Julius Kirshner (London and New York: Longmans, 1988). The chapter is number seven, entitled "Tridentine Reform," and is a rich description of religious revival in sixteenth-century Italy, replete with references to the

Italian sources Cochrane knew so well. Like Evennett's *The Spirit of the Counter-Reformation,* it can complement this present offering.

JOHN C. OLIN
Professor Emeritus

Fordham University
July 31, 1989

ABBREVIATIONS

CHR[3]   *Christian Humanism and the Reformation: Selected Writings of Erasmus.* Ed. John C. Olin. 3rd ed. New York: Fordham University Press, 1987.

CR   John C. Olin. *The Catholic Reformation: Savonarola to Ignatius Loyola.* New York: Harper & Row, 1969.

Evennett   H. Outram Evennett. *The Spirit of the Counter-Reformation.* Ed. John Bossy. Cambridge: Cambridge University Press, 1968.

Jedin   Hubert Jedin. *A History of the Council of Trent* I–II. Trans. Dom Ernest Graf, o.s.b. St. Louis: B. Herder, 1957, 1961.

Pastor   Ludwig Pastor. *The History of the Popes from the Close of the Middle Ages.* Trans. F. I. Antrobus, R. F. Kerr, et al. 40 vols. St. Louis: B. Herder, 1891–1953.

Schroeder *Canons and Decrees of the Council of Trent.* Trans. H. J. Schroeder. St. Louis: B. Herder, 1941.

ILLUSTRATIONS

1 Cardinal Francisco Ximenes de Cisneros (1436–1517), archbishop of Toledo and primate of Spain. From a contemporary etching.

2 A page from Volume I of the Complutensian Polyglot Bible, showing the text of Genesis 1:24–2:1.

3 *The Council of Trent*, a painting by Titian, now in the Louvre.

4 The title page of a published decree granting safe-conduct to the German Protestants invited to attend the Council of Trent. The decree was published in 1562 at Riva by Pietro Antonio Alciati, a local printer regularly used by the Council Fathers.

The Illustrations are between pages 44 and 45.

CATHOLIC REFORM

Catholic Reform
from Cardinal Ximenes
to the Council of Trent

THE INITIAL QUESTION that may well arise in a study of this sort is why the great concern about religious reform in the early sixteenth century—why the widespread search, the urgent demand, the efforts to achieve it—and why, to be sure, the crisis of the Reformation that occurred at this time. There is certainly more than one question involved here, and a single definitive response can hardly be given. The conventional approach in replying has been that there were serious ills and abuses in the Church and that these required correction and reform. A litany of troubles and deficiencies can easily be compiled. It will range from worldly Renaissance popes and prelates to ignorant, unworthy priests and friars, and cover such objectionable practices as the selling of indulgences and the buying of church office, and it will include sins of omission as well as sins of commission. It will run the gamut from theological confusion and desiccation in the academy to gross superstition in religious practice at the popular level. Erasmus in his day laid most of these evils bare, and historians continue to enumerate them and stress their baleful presence and effect. There is also another approach in explaining the extensive phenomenon of reform in the sixteenth century, more popular now perhaps than the older conventional one but not entirely exclusive of it. It is that the times were changing rapidly and

radically and almost in every respect and that the Church itself
was being affected and challenged and impelled to respond. Under
these circumstances reform becomes less a correction of abuses
than an adaptation to new conditions and needs and an effort
toward greater relevance and renewal.

This approach was heralded in a famous essay by Lucien Febvre
entitled "Une question mal posée: Les origines de la réforme
française et le problème des causes de la réforme" that appeared in
the *Revue historique* in 1929.[1] Febvre's main contention was that
the coming of the Reformation is a question not of the reform of
abuses in the Church but rather of a search for a more vital and
relevant Christianity—for a more meaningful faith than the old
Church was offering to the bourgeoisie. He saw everywhere in the
early sixteenth century "a profound need for moral and religious
renewal." Variations on this theme are numerous and are generally
in line with the specific preoccupation or point of view of the
individual historian. Steven Ozment, for example, treating reform
from the standpoint of the Protestant revolt, emphasizes "the
failure of the late medieval Church to provide a theology and
spirituality that could satisfy and discipline religious hearts and
minds."[2] He asserts, however, that "the road to the Reformation
was paved both by unprecedented abuse and a long-unsatisfied
popular religious yearning." Thus he joins both the old and the
new approach to the problem of the Reformation's origins. H.
Outram Evennett, on the other hand, focusing on the continuation
and adaptation of Catholicism in the sixteenth century, concen-
trates on its constructive response to the times and on positive
achievements within the Catholic Church.[3] This discrepancy at
least in part is a matter of the difference in subject each author is
dealing with, though differences of personal view and background
may also play a role.

There is a growing tendency, however, to view the Protestant
and Catholic Reformations as two parallel reform movements or,
to quote Evennett, as "two different, contemporaneous, and ulti-
mately self-subsistent modes of religious and ecclesiastical reform
arising out of the aspirations and confusions and uncertainties of
the early sixteenth century."[4] Lucien Febvre indicates as much—
his thesis indeed implies it—though his focus is on the origin of
Protestant reform, whereas Evennett, who also sees the Protestant

and Catholic movements developing out of the same context, is concerned solely with Catholic reform. The French scholar Jean Delumeau advances a similar theme. His volume bears the title (in its English edition) *Catholicism Between Luther and Voltaire: A New View of the Counter-Reformation,* but he posits the existence of two Reformations, two complementary aspects of a very broad effort toward religious renewal and reform.[5] His thesis (he has called it an hypothesis) is that in the Middle Ages the average person was only superficially Christianized. Pagan and animistic survivals persisted, and the Church was seriously deficient in its pastoral mission. In due time there came an awakening at least in the towns, and new religious demands were made. "In this context the two Reformations, Luther's and Rome's, were two processes, which apparently competed but in actual fact converged, by which the masses were christianized and religion spiritualized." But Delumeau's main concern is with the Catholic Reformation, that is, with "the positive and innovatory aspects, the richness and energy, of Tridentine Catholicism," as he tells us in his Foreword. His subject thus is akin to Evennett's, though the scope of his study and his analysis are quite different. Using the old label "Counter-Reformation" in his case as in Evennett's is confusing and misleading.

Be that as it may, it is undeniable that singular circumstances and demands confronted the Church at the turn of the sixteenth century and that an extraordinary era of religious ferment, activity, and reform now began. The times, marked as they were by geographical discovery and expansion, by heightened economic and political change, and by such innovations as the invention and rapid spread of printing, unquestionably quickened and challenged man's religious consciousness. "The age was one of astonishing religious creativity," in the words of Professor Eugene Rice, "pullulating with saints, mystics, reformers, and original theologians."[6] Perhaps we can best understand the situation in terms of Catholic reform if we examine some of the major efforts in that direction that were undertaken at this time. Criticisms made as well as remedies proposed and measures achieved will reveal much about the state of the Church and the quality of religious life—at least as contemporaries observed and appraised conditions—and also, of course, about the changes they desired.

Taking the year 1495 as a point of departure, let us turn then to the actual historical scene.

A single event can set the stage. On January 13, 1495, Fra Girolamo Savonarola, prior of the Dominican convent of San Marco, preached a sermon in the Duomo in Florence on the renovation of the Church. He described the evils of the time, called for repentance and reform—"O Italy, O princes of Italy, O prelates of the Church, the wrath of God is over you, and you will not have any cure unless you mend your ways!"—and saw punishment at hand, but prophesied also the eventual renewal of the Church.[7] Savonarola was a forceful charismatic preacher with a prophetic message, and he spoke now to a city that had just witnessed the collapse of the Medici regime and to an Italy plunged into turmoil because of the invasion of the peninsula by Charles VIII of France. The times were troubled indeed, and his message as well as his career were bound up in the events that were now occurring. They have also a deeper purpose and significance. Savonarola was an authentic religious reformer whose consuming aim was the revival of Christian virtue and Christian faith in what he observed was a wicked age. It was an aspiration shared by many who, like Savonarola, grieved for "the ruin of the Church" and recognized the need for radical reform. Under pressure from a pope whom he came to denounce he was brought to trial and the scaffold in the spring of 1498. "The wicked were stronger than the good," to quote a contemporary judgment, but the memory of his life and the impact of his words by no means disappeared. His voice ringing through the Duomo echoed down the crucial years that followed, and other men in other ways cried his alarm and pursued his goals.

One of these was the cardinal of Spain and chancellor of Castile, Francisco Ximénes de Cisneros. The most important personage in the court of Ferdinand and Isabella, he succeeded Cardinal Mendoza as archbishop of Toledo, the primatial see, in 1495, and from that post inspired and directed an immense work of ecclesiastical, intellectual, and religious reform. His prominence coincided with the emergence of a united Spain expanding politically, geographically, and intellectually and destined to be the great imperial power of the sixteenth century. He was in his sixtieth year when he became archbishop and entered the most active phase of his long career. Before that, after studies at Salamanca and in Italy, he had been a secular priest, an able church administrator, and from 1484 on an austere Franciscan friar. In 1492 he reluctantly accepted the office of confessor to Queen Isabella, and in 1494 he was appointed provincial of the Franciscans in Castile and initiated reforms in the order. As archbishop and primate he aimed more broadly at restoring the discipline of the diocesan clergy and revitalizing the Church's pastoral mission. In synods at Alcalá in 1497 and Talavera in 1498 he set down the program his priests must follow: they must reside in their parishes, they must refrain from concubinage, they must go to confession frequently, they must preach the Gospel to their people, they must instruct the young. In 1499 he began to lay plans to establish a new university at Alcalá for the education of a more competent and dedicated clergy, a clergy who would constitute, in the words of Marcel Bataillon, "the cadres of a Church more worthy of Christ."[8] Its first college, San Ildefonso, was opened in 1508, and in addition to scholastic theology Greek and Hebrew were taught, making it the first in a line of trilingual colleges that now began to appear throughout Europe.

Alcalá from the start was the center of humanism in Spain, and the work of Ximenes, with its emphasis on education and scholarship, is a striking example of the association between humanism and actual Church reform. Humanism, derived from the expression *studia humanitatis*, is the name given to the so-called classical revival, the renewed study of the literature of ancient Rome and Greece, in Renaissance Italy. It encompassed also a renewed interest in and a more comprehensive and scholarly approach to the scriptural and patristic sources of Europe's faith. It provided thus both a stimulus and a means for religious renewal and reform. I shall have occasion frequently to discuss and exemplify this movement and emphasize its importance, but nowhere is the nexus between Renaissance humanism and reform more clearly seen than in the case of Ximenes. The whole thrust and character of his efforts at Alcalá demonstrate it. He gathered there an array of distinguished scholars—Antonio de Nebrija, Hernán Núñez, Demetrios Doucas of Crete, Alonso de Zamora, and many others, all pioneers of the new learning in Spain. They taught at the university and worked as well on the great edition of Holy

Scripture in its original languages known as the Complutensian Polyglot Bible (Complutum was the Latin name for Alcalá) that was prepared under Ximenes' sponsorship and direction.[9] This latter project including both Old and New Testaments was begun in 1502 and completed in 1517, a short time before Ximenes died, and is one of the great achievements both of humanist scholarship and of early printing. It comprised six folio volumes and was printed at Alcalá in the years 1513 to 1517, though actual publication was delayed until 1522. Its Greek and Latin New Testament volume was the first one through the press, and its colophon bears the date January 10, 1514, which makes it the first Greek New Testament ever printed. Ximenes dedicated this landmark work to Pope Leo X, expressing the hope that "the hitherto dormant study of Holy Scripture may now at last begin to revive." Ximenes' dedicatory preface is in the document section of this volume, and I have also reproduced a page from one of the Complutensian's Old Testament volumes as an illustration to indicate the level of scholarship as well as of typographical skill the work embodies.

Several other notable works had been printed at Alcalá prior to the great Polyglot. A press had been established there as early as 1502, and its first book was a Castilian version of a medieval classic, Ludolph of Saxony's *Life of Christ*. It was this book that Ignatius Loyola read in 1521 as he convalesced from his battle wounds and that played a part in his religious conversion. It is the first of several links between Ximenes and the founder of the Jesuits, an historical relationship deserving close attention. In 1511 the printer of the Complutensian Polyglot, Arnao Guillen de Brocar, established himself at Alcalá and under Ximenes' auspices promptly brought out an edition of Savonarola's commentary on Psalm 50, the *Miserere mei,* and of George of Trebizond's *Rhetoric,* works also pointing to interesting linkages, it seems fair to say. In the dynamic Spain of Cardinal Ximenes a reform pattern of many strands meets the eye. It is not surprising that historians have advanced a "Spanish thesis" to mark and explain the beginnings of Catholic reform in this age.[10] But Spain was an integral part of a larger Christendom and an expanding power of the first magnitude at the turn of the sixteenth century and was influenced greatly by events and currents in the world outside. Italy especially was a prime attraction, and the scholarly interest there in antiquity and its languages and literature had major effect. This humanism to an impressive extent guided Ximenes' reforms.

To appreciate this influence one has to dismiss the notion that Renaissance humanism arose as a cultural, literary, or philosophical movement in opposition to Christian values and beliefs. Jacob Burckhardt's *Civilization of the Renaissance in Italy* enshrined that view more than a century ago, but it is now generally seen as misleading and untenable. In fact a contrary evaluation is much closer to the mark. Humanism now more frequently is viewed as a regenerative or revival movement within the context of the classical *and Christian* tradition and as including a renewed interest in the literature of Christian antiquity—Scripture and the early Fathers—as well as in the pagan literature of Rome and Greece.[11] This extended humanism is often called Christian humanism and associated with later northern humanists like Erasmus, but there was also a religious and reformative thrust in the earlier humanism of Italy as the work of many Italian scholars makes clear—Ambrogio Traversari, Gianozzo Manetti, Lorenzo Valla, to mention three of the most outstanding. By the sixteenth century Renaissance humanism was beginning to have a galvanizing effect throughout Europe, and a return to Holy Scripture and the Fathers was seen more and more as a means of reforming theology and revivifying Christian life. The undertakings of Ximenes and Spanish humanists like Antonio de Nebrija, of course, represent this current in Spain, but everywhere there were signs now of a comparable influence and awareness.

In 1496, for example, John Colet, the English scholar, theologian, and future dean of St. Paul's, began lecturing on the Epistles of St. Paul at Oxford, employing the grammatical and historical method of the humanists and giving new meaning and relevance to the sacred text. He had just returned from several years of study in France and Italy, and it would appear that under the influence of the Florentine Platonists and of Savonarola he had come back to England an ardent reformer. His Oxford lectures directed toward both theological reform and religious revival stirred wide attention and are particularly noteworthy because of their influence on Erasmus. The great Dutch humanist first visited England in 1499 on the eve of his own career and met Colet, with whom he began a long and close friendship, at Oxford. He was deeply

impressed by Colet's labors and commended him for doing battle
with the modern theologians and attempting to restore the true
theology of the ancient Church—the *vetus ac vera theologia*, as he
called it.[12] Colet wanted him to join him in this task and to lecture
on the Old Testament, but Erasmus for the time being declined.
He promised, however, that "as soon as I feel myself to possess
the necessary stamina and strength, I shall come personally to join
your party, and will give devoted, if not distinguished, service in
the defence of theology." It was a pledge he thoroughly and
completely fulfilled.

With Erasmus of Rotterdam we encounter the "prince of humanists" and the most important exponent of reform in the
Christian humanist tradition.[13] A young and talented Augustinian
canon, he had left his monastery and native Holland in 1493 to
enter the service of the bishop of Cambrai, and in 1495 he came
to Paris to study theology and make contact with the wider world
of letters and learning. His visit to England in 1499 marked a
turning point in his life and is the prelude to an extremely
productive career as a scholar and author that extends from the
publication of the first edition of his *Adagia* in 1500 to his death in
1536. It is a career of intense dedication and ceaseless labor in
behalf of the causes he espoused, and the merit of his work as well
as his enormous output won him a stature and influence rivaled
by few other scholars and authors in European history.

What were the causes Erasmus espoused? In a letter of October
1527 he gave this summary account:

> I have vigorously raised my voice against the wars which we see
> for so many years now agitating nearly all of Christendom. I have
> attempted to call back theology, sunk too far in sophistical quib-
> bling, to the sources and to ancient simplicity. I have sought to
> restore to their own splendor the sacred doctors of the Church. . . .
> I have taught good literature, previously nearly pagan, to celebrate
> Christ. I have supported to the best of my ability the blossoming
> of languages once again.[14]

It is a fair description of his endeavors which we can paraphrase
and supplement by emphasizing that the primary aim of Erasmus
was reform—the reform of theology through a return to Scripture
and the Fathers and the reform of Christian life and society as a

consequence of this theological renewal. Practically all his writings and editions in one way or another bear witness to this basic yet comprehensive goal: his *Adagia*; his *Enchiridion militis christiani*; his famous *Praise of Folly*, which he dedicated to Thomas More; his Greek and Latin New Testament, which was published (though not printed) before Cardinal Ximenes' New Testament volume— it was published by Johann Froben in Basel in 1516; his monumental edition of Saint Jerome, the first of his many patristic editions— it also saw the light of day in 1516; his *Colloquies*.

As is clear, Erasmus, though he was the outstanding intellectual personage of his time, was by no means alone in these scholarly and reform endeavors. The work of the great French humanist Jacques Lefèvre d'Etaples, for example, paralleled his own.[15] The latter's scholarly edition of the Psalms, with five variant Latin texts, appeared in 1509; his edition of Saint Paul's Epistles, in 1512; his important *Commentaries on the Four Gospels*, in 1522; and his French translation of the New Testament, in 1523. Lefèvre prefaced these works with introductions of the greatest importance in promoting the course of the scriptural revival and inspiring the *évangélisme* he represented. He was also actively engaged from 1521 to 1525 in the administration and reform of a diocese in France—the bishopric of Meaux, then headed by his lifelong friend and patron Guillaume Briçonnet. Lefèvre's efforts were compromised and made suspect by the rise of Protestantism in the 1520s, and the Meaux circle that centered around him was dispersed in 1525; but like Erasmus, Colet, and Ximenes, he must properly be acknowledged as a leader in a movement aimed at Catholic renewal and reform.

One can indeed ask whether the thrust of this movement was authentically Catholic. Did it not pose a danger to the established Church? Did it not in fact, with its scriptural emphasis and exegesis, pave the way for Protestantism and schism? Historians have given a variety of answers to these questions, which arise in the first place because of the deep divisions in Christendom that came after 1517. Similarly the Protestant–Catholic polarization that so rapidly occurred in the midst of the religious crisis and that persisted down through the centuries influenced the attitudes and judgments men expressed. For example, Erasmus from his own time until quite recently has been viewed by many as "laying the egg Luther hatched," and Lefèvre has been seen as a kind of

proto- or crypto-Protestant. The several reformers I have discussed, however, indubitably considered themselves Catholic and
their activities as being within the orbit of the existing Catholic
Church. They strove to reform that Church and its members, not
to defy it or work outside it or create another one in its place. If at
times their methods or their criticisms raised the hackles of the
theologians in the faculties at Paris or Louvain—the scholastic or
the *modern* theologians, as Erasmus called them—or the ire of
certain monks, that neither excluded them from the Church nor
violated their Catholic faith. The Church after all revered Scripture as the revealed Word of God, "the very storehouse of faith,"
to quote Thomas More, a humanist whom we also venerate as a
martyr for his Catholic beliefs.[16] The humanist approach is now
being more accurately appraised as fully orthodox and in keeping
with the patristic tradition and as aimed at effecting reform within
the existing structure.[17]

But the peaceful and progressive realization of such reform was
not to be. On almost the day of Ximenes' death in 1517 Martin
Luther advanced to the center of the stage, and the great controversy stemming from his Ninety-Five Theses began. I need not
elaborate here on the crisis that now ensued or apportion praise or
blame for the events that followed. Suffice it to say that the Church
was rent, the authority of the pope overthrown in many lands,
and important aspects of the doctrine and religious practice of
centuries disputed and denied. However one appraises the role of
Luther or analyzes the causes of the widespread revolt that now
occurred, it is clear that the historical Catholic Church was newly
and most gravely challenged and that its very life was cast into the
balance. A very complex pattern of Catholic activity developed.
There was obviously a response to the Protestant challenge:
traditional Catholic doctrine was to be defended, heresy con-
demned, the revolt checked and suppressed, the Church maintained and restored. This reflexive or defensive movement we are
accustomed to calling the Counter-Reformation, a term that originated with the German historian Ranke more than a century and
a half ago. The earlier concern for renewal and reform also
continued, yet clearly the scene had radically changed after 1517.

For one thing a reform of abuses and shortcomings in the
Church became all the more urgent as men witnessed the "trag-

edy" that had occurred. "God permits this persecution to afflict His Church," declared Pope Adrian VI in 1522, "because of the sins of men, especially of the priests and prelates of the Church."[18] And he pledged himself to "expend every effort to reform first this Curia, whence perhaps all this evil has come, so that, as corruption spread from that place to every lower place, the good health and reformation of all may also issue forth. We consider ourselves all the more bound to attend to this," he continued, "the more we perceive the entire world longing for such a reformation." It was a point of view shared by many and voiced again most notably by Cardinal Reginald Pole in his opening address at the Council of Trent.[19] Certain features of Catholic reform prior to 1517, however, became either suspect or inappropriate or more difficult to sustain as religious controversy widened and positions became more rigid and extreme. Erasmus' sharp criticism of the monks, for example, and the pious and somewhat mystical *évangélisme* of Lefèvre seemed all the more dangerous and subversive in their opponents' eyes under the conditions that now prevailed. Erasmus himself said that, had he foreseen what was coming, he would not have written certain things or he would have expressed himself in a different way. Nevertheless ongoing currents of reform survived, and signs of positive spiritual revival quite independent of the religious crisis or the schism persisted and multiplied in the Catholic fold. One of the chief evidences of this revival is the formation of many new religious orders in the period after 1517, the Theatines, the Capuchins, the Jesuits, to name three of the most important ones.[20] And these new orders serve not merely as signs of a religious awakening or of vitality within Catholicism; they were instruments for further reform in the Church, and the Jesuits in particular were active in its now far-flung missionary endeavors.

Catholic spirituality at this time was highly individualistic and activist, in contrast to the more communal and contemplative spirituality of the Middle Ages. The stress was on the individual's interior religious experience—on private prayer and meditation, self-discipline, personal sanctification and spiritual growth— rather than on community devotions and formal liturgical piety. "Surely, we see here," Evennett observes, "the individualism of the age taking its appropriate form in Catholic spirituality."[21] The heightened "personalization" of the religious impulse had an exterior side as well, expressing itself—overflowing, so to speak—in a more intense active life. This took numerous forms: a literature prescribing religious *exercises* (the term itself is revealing), a deep concern with conduct and with moral or ethical questions, an emphasis on the virtue of charity, the desire to be of service to others, the renewal of the pastoral ministry, missionary zeal and endeavor. "Love ought to manifest itself in deeds rather than in words," St. Ignatius Loyola wrote in his *Spiritual Exercises*, and this principle, appearing in a famous book of exercises for "the conquest of self and the regulation of one's life," expresses as well as any other single statement the nature and thrust of the new spirituality. Indeed Ignatius' whole life—his conversion, his labors and apostolate, his *Spiritual Exercises*, his injunction to seek God in all things—exemplifies in classic form his spirituality which in the course of the sixteenth century was to enliven and renew the Catholic Church.

This new spirituality was prefigured by currents in the fifteenth century such as the *Devotio Moderna* in northern Europe and the devout humanism of so many Italian scholars, and Erasmus reveals its most salient features. In his *Enchiridion militis christiani* (or *Handbook of the Christian Soldier*), written in 1501, he expresses a personal inward piety, completely Christocentric, that must manifest itself not in outward ceremonial or legalistic observance but in charity and the moral life. This attitude was drawn from Holy Scripture, but it was also formed by the moralistic tendencies of the *Devotio Moderna* and the spiritualizing influence of Renaissance Platonism. It remained throughout Erasmus' life the very core of his religious thought.

A similar spirituality can be seen at work in the lay religious societies or confraternities that existed in Italy in the late fifteenth and early sixteenth centuries, notably in the Genoese and Roman Oratories of Divine Love. The Genoese Oratory was founded in 1497 by a prominent layman, Ettore Vernazza, inspired by a remarkable woman then in charge of a hospital in Genoa, the very practical-minded mystic known as St. Catherine of Genoa.[22] The Oratory was a predominantly lay association whose members sought to cultivate their spiritual lives through the faithful practice of religious devotions and works of charity and benevolence, specifically assistance to one another in times of need and the care of the sick. "Our fraternity," their charter begins, "is not instituted for any other purpose than to root and implant in our hearts divine love, that is to say, charity." Sometime prior to 1517 another Oratory, patterned after the Genoese society, was established in Rome, an event that historians have often singled out at marking the beginning of effective Catholic reform because of the number of prominent reformers who were associated with it.[23] These include Gaetano da Thiene, a devout priest and curial official, later canonized; Gian Pietro Carafa, bishop of Chieti and papal diplomat who subsequently reigned as Pope Paul IV; and several other notable figures whose names will become familiar in the pages that follow. Even Guillaume Briçonnet, whom I have mentioned as bishop of Meaux and Lefèvre's patron, and who was on embassy in Rome in the years 1516 to 1518, is said to have come under its influence.

Oratories were established in other Italian cities, but the most important extension of this development perhaps was an offshoot of the Roman Oratory, a new religious order known as the Theatines, the pioneer of several new orders of priests actively engaged in pastoral and charitable work.[24] The Theatines were founded in 1524 by da Thiene and Carafa and two other members of the Roman Oratory and represent a more permanent and structured expression of the Oratory's ideal, that is, one for priests who would live in community under a rule and undertake an active apostolate. The term Theatine, derived from Carafa's bishopric of Chieti or Theate, soon became synonymous in Italy with an austere and reformed priesthood.

After the devastating sack of Rome by mutinous imperial troops in May 1527, the Theatines, then numbering fourteen members with Carafa their first superior, took refuge in Venice where they continued their work and had close ties with the eminent Venetian noble and humanist Gasparo Contarini, and with the reforming bishop in nearby Verona, Gian Matteo Giberti. The names of both Contarini and Giberti have traditionally been associated with the earlier Roman Oratory, but they will be linked more firmly henceforth with that of Carafa in the general movement of Catholic reform. In Venice Carafa became deeply concerned at the

laxity and disorder of the Venetian Church and at the spread of
heresy in the great maritime republic. His concerns, which he
expressed in an appeal to Pope Clement VII in 1532, reveal all too
well the problems that now confronted the Catholic reformers.[25]
They were dealing not only with the correction of abuses in the
Church and the renewal of pastoral activity and religious life but
also with the rising tide. of heresy and revolt. These separate
problems, although interrelated, evoked their specific remedies
and counter-measures. The tensions and dilemmas of Catholic
reform and the so-called Counter-Reformation now began to
appear. During these years the Theatines remained a small but
influential order. They set new standards for the priesthood in
Italy and furnished many bishops for the Church. They signaled a
sorely needed revitalization of the Church's pastoral mission.

The Capuchin order was founded in Italy about the same time
as the Theatines. Very different in inspiration and background, the
order originated in 1525 with the decision of a young Franciscan
Observant, Matteo da Bascio, to leave his friary in the Marches of
Ancona to lead a solitary life in more strict and faithful accordance
with the Rule of St. Francis of Assisi.[26] He was soon joined by
other Franciscan Observants. The Capuchins, named after their
square hood or *cappuccio*, were not the first to attempt to return to
the primitive simplicity and poverty of St. Francis—they were in
the tradition of the Spirituals—but they were perhaps the most
successful, and their emergence at this time is a striking manifes-
tation of the forces making for religious revival in the sixteenth
century. Although they were confined to Italy until 1574, their
growth was phenomenal: they numbered some seven hundred
members by 1536, when definitive constitutions were drawn up
and Pope Paul III confirmed the order, and their membership
continued to expand rapidly. Grouped chiefly in small hermitages,
they followed a strict life of penance and prayer, though they
devoted themselves also to the work of preaching the Gospel and
caring for the sick and poor. Their evangelical inspiration is
particularly noteworthy and can be related to the broad movement
of scriptural revival. Their constitutions stressed that they "must
always bear the holy Gospel in the interior of their hearts" and
read and study Holy Scripture and preach the Gospel "so that

being evangelical preachers, they may fashion an evangelical people."

The early expansion of the Capuchin order was attended by certain difficulties, particularly the hostility of the Observant authorities who saw it as a rebellion in their own ranks and a standing criticism. The apostasy of their fourth vicar general, Bernadino Ochino, the greatest preacher in Italy of his day, and his flight to Calvin's Geneva in 1542 were another severe trial that almost led to the order's destruction. But the significance of Ochino's flight extended beyond the Capuchin movement. Dramatizing the thrust and danger of Protestantism in Italy, it coincided with the establishment of a restructured and more effective inquisition at Rome under Carafa's direction in 1542.[27] Its task was to examine and try those suspected of heresy, and Ochino, as well as his friend Peter Martyr Vermigli, the Augustinian prior at Lucca, had been summoned before it. (This Roman Inquisition, which was confined to Italy and was occasioned by the alarming spread of Protestant doctrines there, should not be confused with the more notorious Spanish Inquisition, which dated from 1478 and operated in Spain under royal auspices. The latter was directed savagely against suspected Jewish converts, the *conversos*, when it was set up, although later it too became an arm of the Counter-Reformation.)

At this same time in the summer of 1542 there occurred the sudden death of Cardinal Gasparo Contarini who had headed the more liberal reform party at the papal court and represented a more conciliatory attitude toward Protestantism. The coincidence of these three events has frequently been viewed as a major turning point in the Catholic Reformation, the point at which spirits cleft and a far more repressive and intransigent attitude began to dominate the Catholic scene. The Inquisition took over, and the fiery Carafa replaced the more moderate Contarini in ascendancy at Rome.[28] The defection of Ochino in a sense triggered this transition. One should guard however against too simplistic an analysis of these events or too exaggerated a notion of an abrupt change in the movement of Catholic reform. Each of the events I have discussed is important, but the gradual evolution of Catholic attitudes during these difficult and critical years and other circumstances also affecting the course of reform loom even larger on the historical stage.

The work and influence of Gian Matteo Giberti, bishop of Verona, is a case in point.[29] Born in Palermo in 1495, he first came to Rome in 1513 to become a secretary to Cardinal Giulio de Medici. When that prelate was elected Pope Clement VII in 1523, Giberti served as his most trusted minister and adviser. He was a friend of da Thiene's and Carafa's and a staunch supporter of the early Theatines. After the sack of Rome in 1527, he withdrew to the see of Verona where he had previously been appointed bishop, and he resided there until his death in 1543. His residence and reforms there also associate him with Contarini and other like-minded reformers in the Venetian Republic, and he was a friend of Ochino, who was in Verona when he received his summons to Rome in 1542. He has been called "the bishop *par excellence* of the Catholic reform." He truly cared for his flock and saw that worthy men served as priests and that they preached the Gospel and instructed the young. He established a society for the relief of the poor, and he founded an *accademia* for scholars and poets. By his own life, as contemporaries were quick to observe, he set the best example, and both his example and his reforms had wide influence. His diocesan regulations, the *Constitutiones Gibertinae*, which were published in 1542 and again in 1563, served as a pattern for many of the reforms of the Council of Trent.

In weighing the significance of Giberti it must be stressed that the restoration of the bishop's role and responsibility was one of the most pressing needs of the Church at this time. Many of its ills stemmed from the fact that all too many bishops were non-resident—Contarini called it "the calamity of our age"—and oblivious of their pastoral obligations. This problem was one of the main preoccupations of the Catholic reformers, and it later became the focus of some of the most important Tridentine decrees. Progress here is an important measure of Catholic revival. The model or ideal of the good bishop, however, predates Giberti's work in Verona. In 1516 Gasparo Contarini had written a short treatise on the office and duties of the bishop for a friend who had just been appointed to the see of Bergamo.[30] His own model was an exemplary bishop of Padua whom he had known in his student days. Giberti, in fact, was in an ancient tradition.

Contarini's treatise in a sense inaugurates his active career and is evidence that his zeal for reform antecedes the Lutheran controversy and schism and his own service as cardinal and counselor at the court of Paul III. He is one of the most impressive figures in this story of Catholic reform, and his life in many respects—his learning, his political involvements, his nobility of character—calls to mind that of his great English contemporary Thomas More. Born in 1483, he was a member of one of the oldest and most prominent Venetian families. He studied at the University of Padua where he received a thorough grounding in the classics as well as in philosophy and theology. One of his steachers was the noted Renaissance Aristotelian Pietro Pomponazzi, with whom he later took issue on the philosophical question of the immortality of the soul. Contarini himself was a Thomist, a follower of the school of St. Thomas Aquinas, and a humanist, a combination not unusual at this time. After leaving Padua in 1509, he took his seat on the Great Council of Venice, though in 1511 the entry of his close friends Tommaso Giustiniani and Vincenzo Quirini into the Camaldolese Order and their effort to persuade Contarini to join them in the contemplative monastic life occasioned great soul-searching on his part. This coincided with a personal religious crisis not unlike that which Martin Luther was shortly to undergo in his monastery at Wittenberg. Contarini, however, declined the cloister and decided to follow a lay vocation, convinced that active service in the world was not only consonant with deep Christian faith but meritorious and indeed preferable as well.[31] It is against this background that he wrote his treatise on the duties of the bishop and began his career in the public service of his native Venice. He served as ambassador to the court of Emperor Charles V from 1521 to 1525 and later to the papal court. He composed an important political treatise on the government of the Venetian Republic, extolling its well-ordered constitution and the ideal principles underlying it. Felix Gilbert speculates that it may have been a reply to the *Utopia* of Thomas More whom he once had met on a diplomatic mission in Bruges.[32]

In the 1530s Contarini was a prominent member of what may be called the Venetian reform circle and was made a cardinal and called to Rome by Paul III, but before I discuss this phase of his career I should like to call attention to a very comprehensive

reform program drafted by his friends Giustiniani and Quirini
shortly after they entered the religious life. It is not amiss to link
Contarini with their aims and proposals. The two Camaldolese
monks presented their memorial in 1513 to the Medici Pope Leo
X, who had recently been elected, and it is known as the *Libellus
ad Leonem X.*[33] They looked hopefully to the new pope in the
context of the Fifth Lateran Council, which was then in session,
to give strong leadership in the reform of the Church.[34] The
Libellus stressed the role of the pope and his authority in a
restructured and revitalized Church administration. Cardinals
were to be his assistants (and supported solely by a monthly
salary), bishops to be closely supervised, clergy to be carefully
selected and adequately trained. General Councils were to be
convened every five years, and provincial and diocesan synods
were to be held periodically. Canon law was to be revised, Holy
Scripture to be translated into the vernacular, the liturgy to be
simplified and made uniform, superstition to be rooted out. "It is
no exaggeration to say," declares Hubert Jedin, "that the reform
program of the two Camaldolese monks preoccupied the Church
for more than a century." And it rings, I think we can say, even
more distant bells. Neither pope nor Council fulfilled their immediate hopes however, though many of their ideas will be echoed
and some at least implemented in the troubled years ahead.

As I have already indicated, there was a circle of ardent reformers in Venice and vicinity that included Contarini, Carafa, and
Giberti. Prominent also was the abbot of the Benedictine monastery of San Giorgio Maggiore in Venice, Gregorio Cortese.
Cortese, who was elected abbot of the Venetian monastery in
1532, had long been active in the reform of the Italian Benedictines, and his efforts in this regard are especially noteworthy
because of the emphasis he placed on the renewal of study and the
pursuit of learning as means to this end.[35] He illustrates once again
that connection between humanism and reform I have previously
observed. Joining this group in the 1530s was a young English
noble, Reginald Pole. A cousin of Henry VIII's, he had earlier
been a student at Padua, and opposed to the divorce proceedings
in which the English king was now so deeply involved, he
returned to Italy in 1532 desirous of continuing his studies. His
scholarly and religious concerns brought him into close associa-

tion with the Venetian circle, and their influence shaped the rest of his life.[36] In May 1535 Contarini, still a layman, quite unexpectedly was apppointed a cardinal and summoned to Rome by the newly elected Paul III. Taking up residence in the Vatican, he became one of the Pope's closest advisers. The others were soon to join him at the papal court.

It is at this point in 1535 when Paul III brought Gasparo Contarini to Rome that the Counter-Reformation in one sense of the word may be said to have begun. Under the aegis of the new pope the Catholic Church now began to put its house in order, in full recognition of the religious crisis that was underway, and the disparate efforts of Catholic reformers began to coalesce. This movement was directed toward reform and was also in its new character and shape generated by the very serious challenges that had come. Hence there is some justification for calling it a counter reformation. This is a departure from the traditional meaning of the term, but given the inadequacy of the old concept of Counter-Reformation it may well be a more suitable application of the time-honored phrase. The summoning of Contarini to Rome by the pope can be seen as the inauguration of this development because it represents the conjunction of papal initiative and leadership with reform. Both men were outstanding individuals, and their union in a common cause, despite all the difficulties and setbacks, heralded a new day for the Catholic Church. A turning point had been reached.

Paul III, the former Cardinal Alessandro Farnese and dean of the College of Cardinals, was elected pope in late 1534, and his pontificate, the longest of the century, extended until late 1549.[37] He was a wily, intelligent, and seasoned Renaissance prelate in whom the old and unsavory habits of the papal prince contended with the demands of these troubled and perilous times, but these demands now at least were heard and a serious response was made. From the start he sought to convene the General Council that so many desired, and he finally assembled it at Trent in December 1545. From the start he grappled with the stubborn problems of curial reform, though less than effectively. "He talked but he didn't act," judged the Augustinian General Girolamo Seripando. It was he who commissioned Michelangelo to paint the gigantic altarpiece of the Sistine Chapel, *The Last Judgment*. This tremendous work, begun in 1536 and completed in 1541, echoing the prophetic message of Savonarola embodies the vision of a world in judgment. It can be said to epitomize this era of crisis and to express profoundly its anguish as well as its faith.[38] Paul III established the Jesuits in 1539–1540 and dispatched them on their first missions. He reorganized the Roman Inquisition in 1542 and broadened its jurisdiction to deal more effectively with the spread of heresy in Italy. Above all he brought many of the most able and dedicated Catholic reformers to Rome and thereby infused new life and leadership into the papal adminstration. It is his "undying merit," says Jedin, "that these reform groups were able to organize themselves in Rome."[39]

The elevation of Contarini began this salutary process. It was at his suggestion that Paul III, in view of the projected General Council (which the pope had scheduled to meet in Mantua in May 1537) as well as the urgent need to undertake fundamental reform, convened a reform commission in Rome in 1536. Its members for the most part formed a roster of some of the most prominent men in the story of Catholic reform and included first and foremost those friends of Contarini I have previously discussed: Carafa, Giberti, Cortese, and Pole. Four others were also invited to participate: Jacopo Sadoleto, bishop of Carpentras and a noted scholar and former papal secretary,[40] Federigo Fregoso, bishop of Gubbio, the Dominican Tommaso Badia, the papal theologian, and Jerome Aleander, archbishop of Brindisi and papal nuncio. In December 1536 Paul III conferred a cardinal's hat on Carafa, Pole, and Sadoleto. The commission sat for nearly four months and in March 1537 formally presented its report to the pope. This is the famous *Consilium de emendanda ecclesia*, one of the most important documents in our story.[41] It attacked curial practices that had permitted—indeed produced—corruption and mismanagement in the Church and called for the correction of many specific "abuses" so that the Church's pastoral ministry could be properly discharged. Better men must be selected for the episcopacy and for the priesthood, bishops and priests must reside in their churches and care for the faithful, lax religious orders must be abolished, Rome itself must be made an example rather than a scandal to those who see it. It particularly assailed the venality and simony

involved in papal appointments and benefice-holding and attributed these evils to an exaggerated concept of papal authority.
"From this source," it boldly declared, "as from a Trojan horse so
many abuses and such grave diseases have rushed in upon the
Church of God that we now see her afflicted almost to the despair
of salvation. . . . ." And it emphasized throughout the command
of Christ: "Freely you have received, freely give." In conclusion it
appealed to the pope for action: "we hope that you have been
chosen to restore in our hearts and in our works the name of
Christ now forgotten by the nations and by us clerics, to heal the
ills, to lead back the sheep of Christ into one fold, to turn away
from us the wrath of God and that vengeance we deserve, already
prepared and looming over our heads."

The frankness and vigor of its attack and acknowledgment of
guilt are startling indeed and recall the words of Pope Adrian VI
in 1522 that I quoted earlier in this essay. Catholic reformers at
this time had a lively awareness of the responsibility of the papacy
and of prelates and clerics in general for the disaster that had
occurred, and they saw prompt and radical reform as essential per
se and the necessary road to reunion and survival. Michelangelo's
great figure of Christ in judgment was no mere aesthetic conceit.
Unfortunately Paul III did not respond with energy and dispatch
to the recommendations of the *Consilium*, though their automatic
enactment and the immediate *emendatio* of curial practice and
ecclesiastical administration were hardly to be expected, given the
deep-seated evils that prevailed. Too established, too ingrained
were the procedures and the habits that the commission de-
nounced. Its report nevertheless provided an authoritative analysis
and program, raised the banner of reform at Rome, and helped
prepare the way for eventual correction and improvement. The
Church under the pope was beginning to show signs of constructive movement.

Cardinal Contarini also played a part in another significant event
that relates to our story during this time: an attempt to resolve the
schism in Germany through a conference of Protestant and Catholic theologians at Ratisbon (or Regensburg) in 1541.[42] The conference was held in conjunction with a meeting of the Imperial
Diet and was the climax of an effort by the Emperor Charles V to
bring about a reconciliation between Lutherans and Catholics

through such discussion. Paul III sent Contarini as his representa-
tive to head the Catholic delegation, and as an advocate of reunion
no one was more highly regarded or better qualified. The high
point of the conference was an agreement reached on the basic
question of justification, the very issue that Luther had originally
raised and that was central to his theology and to all early
Protestantism. Luther had insisted that men were saved not by
their works but by their faith in a merciful God who gratuitously
imputes justice to the sinner. The Catholic response in general,
like Erasmus' argument in his *De libero arbitrio*, which he wrote in
1524 to confute Luther, sought to preserve man's freedom and
moral responsibility in the justification process. At the Ratisbon
conference Contarini and the other theologians agreed to a compromise formulation called "double justification." It held that any
inherent justification man himself attained had to be supplemented
by a divinely *imputed* justification if he was to be saved. The idea
had been put forward earlier by Johann Gropper as a means toward
effecting reunion, but at the conference Contarini in particular is
credited with advancing it and winning agreement to the compromise. His own personal religious crisis back in 1511 enabled him
to understand more fully the Lutheran insistence on man's depen-
dence on divine grace. The promise of this achievement, however,
was not fulfilled. Agreement on other important theological questions—the doctrine of the Eucharist, for one—was not reached,
and this effort at reunion failed. The division now between Catholicism and Protestantism was too deep. Nor was the notion of
"double justification" sustained by either Rome or Wittenberg.
Carafa and Sadoleto, for example, had misgivings about it from
the start, though the pope took a neutral position. The Fathers at
the Council of Trent after long debate in 1546 rejected the concept
and in their decree on justification laid down a different theology
for the Catholic world.

Meanwhile Ignatius Loyola came to Venice in early 1536, and
his path soon crossed Carafa's and, not long after that, Contarini's. He and several companions who had been students in Paris
had vowed to go to Venice and then on to Jerusalem "where they
would spend their lives in the service of souls." Their enterprise
marks the beginning of the Society of Jesus. It appears that after
his arrival in Venice Ignatius had an encounter with the forceful

Theatine reformer and that differing concepts of the religious life and their respective missions set them at odds.[43] Ignatius' companions, nine in number, joined him in early 1537, and after waiting in vain for nearly a year for a ship to the East (war between Venice and Turks made the prospect unlikely), the band went on to Rome to put themselves at the disposition of the pope. There they met Contarini, who became one of their chief supporters, and thanks to his intervention they gained papal approval for the new order they now formed. This development of decisive importance must be approached, however, not by the way of Carafa or Contarini but through the experience and activity of a Spanish saint.

There are many remarkable individuals in the story of Catholic revival and reform in this period from Cardinal Ximenes to the Council of Trent, as I have observed, but there is none who is more pre-eminent or had greater influence than Ignatius Loyola.[44] He was born Don Iñigo López de Loyola in 1491 to a noble Basque family in the province of Guipuzcoa in the Kingdom of Castile. In his youth he served as a page at the royal court and then as a soldier under the banner of the Spanish kings. In 1517 he entered the service of the Duke of Najera, the Spanish viceroy of Navarre (the Spanish had conquered and annexed that province in 1512), and he was gravely wounded in the spring of 1521 during the seige of Pamplona, the capital of Navarre, at the time of the French invasion. The event was a turning point in his life. He was taken back to the family castle at Loyola to recover from his wounds, and in the months of convalescence that followed he underwent a profound change of heart. Reading of Christ and the saints in the only books available to him, Ludolph of Saxony's *Life of Christ* and Jacopo de Voragine's collection of saints' lives known as *The Golden Legend,* he gave up all thoughts of worldly fame and fortune and resolved to do great deeds as the saints had for the love of God. He is a classic example of a man deeply influenced by what he has read. (The invention of printing in this instance played an important part.) His attention now centered on going to Jerusalem as a penitent pilgrim, and he set off on his journey in early 1522. His travels took him across Spain to the shrine of Our Lady at Montserrat in Catalonia and then to nearby Manresa, where he remained for several months. His experiences

there were of the utmost importance, and he describes them at
some length in his autobiography (Chapter 3). He gained a new
insight into his purpose and vocation and a clearer understanding
of the nature of service under the standard of Christ. He continued
his journey to the Holy Land by way of Rome and Venice in 1523,
but unable to stay there, as he had intended, he returned to Spain
the following year and undertook a long and eventful course of
study. This lasted for more than ten years, from 1524 to 1535,
and took him to Cardinal Ximenes' foundation at Alcalá, then to
the University of Salamanca, and in 1528 to the University of
Paris. He acquired a master of arts degree in Paris in 1534.

Ignatius' Paris years mark a most important phase. These were
years of great ferment and agitation throughout Europe, and
Ignatius could hardly have failed to have been aware of the problems and issues of the world about him. He pursued his studies
nevertheless; his zeal continued; his *Spiritual Exercises*, as they are
called, that well-ordered handbook of meditations, rules, and
practices that stemmed from his own experience, developed.[45]
From the College of Sainte-Barbe, the school he attended in Paris,
he gathered about him the group of companions with whom he
was eventually to form the Society of Jesus. In August 1534
Ignatius and six of his friends, all a great deal younger then he, as
their studies drew to an end, solemnly resolved to go to Jerusalem
to labor for the conversion of the Turks. Among this number were
Francis Xavier of Navarre, a newly ordained priest Pierre Favre of
Savoy, a Portuguese, Simon Rodrigues, and Diego Laynez, a
brilliant student from Castile. Given events in Europe at this time
and the prevailing hostility to the Turks who posed a very serious
threat, it is a most surprising resolve. The pacifist Erasmus, who
often expressed himself on the need to win the Turks to Christ,
would certainly have approved had word of the intention of these
graduates of Sainte-Barbe reached him in his retirement in Freiburg. By the same token their project would seem to indicate that
they were quite oblivious to the internal problems then convulsing
Christendom.

Thus it was that Ignatius and his friends came to Venice and
then, after failing to find a ship to take them to the East, converged
on the Rome of Paul III in 1538. Contarini especially was impressed by their fervor; the pope welcomed and befriended them

and utilized their services. It may well have been his suggestion that they organize more formally as a religious order. The band of ten, as they now numbered, discussed this at length, and in the summer of 1539 drew up a statement of purpose and organization for papal approval.[46] They obtained this and more formal appro- bation in September 1540 in the bull *Regimini militantis ecclesiae*, a delay having been caused by the hesitations of some more con- servative cardinals at the new departure the order represented. Jedin calls their establishment "the first, and perhaps the greatest, success of the reform movement" that was gathering strength in Rome.[47] Meanwhile, new members joined their ranks, and they began to disperse on assignments from the pope. They had bound themselves by a special vow to go wherever he would send them. Favre and Laynez went to Parma for pastoral work; Xavier and Rodrigues went to Portugal at the request of King John III, who wanted missionaries for India;[48] Ignatius was chosen their head or *prepositus*, and he alone of the original band stayed on in Rome to direct the fast-growing society.

By the time of Ignatius' death in July 1556 more than a thousand Jesuits were studying and working in all parts of the world, the earliest and largest community being at Coimbra in Portugal. (Ignatius' letters to the Coimbra Jesuits are among his most important writings.) They engaged in a host of religious and scholarly activities, for from the start they laid great stress on education, and they sought God not in the cloistered contempla- tive life—that was the old monasticism they rejected—but His presence in all things. An intensely active spirituality, as well as a highly personal one, characterized the movement. It seems to have been based on the Erasmian dictum that monasticism in itself is not piety—*monachatus non est pietas*—but rather that a religious life consists of an interior conversion to Christ and active service in His name. "Action was prayer, and prayer led to action," as Evennett has so tersely pointed out.[49] Ignatius himself has been called in a memorable phrase "the contemplative in action." And as "a community founded principally for the advancement of souls in Christian life and doctrine and for the propagation of the faith," they undertook to work for these goals as and where Ignatius (as *prepositus*) or the pope or their successors directed. They were missionaries and theologians, they founded schools and colleges, they strengthened and defended the Catholic cause in divided Germany. There was an unusually large number and wide variety of outstanding individuals in the early society, many of whom were later canonized as saints: Ignatius himself, Francis Xavier, Pierre Favre, Peter Canisius, Francis Borgia only begin the list.

It is hardly necessary to stress that the Jesuits were not founded to combat Protestantism. It is a misrepresentation to picture them as shock troops mustered by a hard-pressed Church to give battle to the heretic. Their militancy was that of "the spiritual combat," a metaphor of ancient Christian origin employed, for example, by Erasmus in his *Enchiridion militis christiani*. But their devotion to the Church made them its staunch defenders. With Ignatius they believed that the Church was the mystical "spouse of Christ," and they saw it as the measure of spiritual authenticity and Christian truth. They saw the pope as Christ's vicar, and they vowed a special obedience to him in matters pertaining to the advancement of souls and the propagation of the faith. Such a perspective is basic to the spirituality and theology of Ignatius and the early Jesuits, and it has profound roots as well as broad significance in terms of the times in which Ignatius lived and the order came into existence. In this sense Ignatius does emerge as the great counter-Luther and the early Jesuits as counter-Protestants. However it was never their intention, their task, or even their achievement simply to defend the Catholic cause against Protestantism. The entire movement, from its inception in the experience of a Spanish *caballero* to the creation and expansion of a new and dynamic order, had a different focus and a deeper and more positive religious purpose.[50]

By the 1540s Erasmus' statement that "the sum and substance of our religion is peace and concord" was far from descriptive of the historical scene, and it barely had meaning any longer as a viable Christian ideal. The schism now cut deep across Europe. Under these circumstances the long-delayed General Council of the Church assembled in December 1545 in the city of Trent, an imperial city just beyond the Brenner Pass on the road to Italy. Jedin believes that a Council should have been convened from the start to deal authoritatively with the Lutheran affair and to inaugurate reform and that its delay was due in the first place to Rome's fear of such an assembly.[51] War in Europe and other political factors also complicated negotiations and led to postponement. Finally, however, Paul III succeeded in his efforts to convene one, and in his bull of convocation of 1542 stressing the dissensions and dangers that existed he exhorted all bishops and princes to attend. The reply was far from unanimous, but the long-awaited assembly opened at last and began its work. We are now at the point when the Catholic Church as an institution took collective action against the ills and perils that beset it. Jedin has called Trent "the Church's answer to the Protestant Reformation." It was indeed the most comprehensive and authoritative response to the crisis that had engulfed it.

The course of the Council was checkered and prolonged. It lasted for eighteen years, until December 1563, though there were lengthy interruptions between sessions. It actually met only in 1545–1547, 1551–1552, and 1562–1563. There were twenty-five formal sessions and innumerable general congregations and committee meetings of bishops and theologians. Representation was always rather limited: some thirty Fathers, mostly Italian, attended the opening on December 13, 1545; some 250 approved and signed its decrees at the closing session on December 3–4, 1563. It was presided over by a series of papal legates, many of them very distinguished men—Reginald Pole, Marcello Cervini,[52] Girolamo Seripando, Stanislaus Hosius, Giovanni Morone. The Protestants, with one minor exception in 1552, refused to attend, viewing it as a council of Antichrist because of its papal sponsorship and direction.[53] Nor was there any real French representation until the final period, at which time the Cardinal of Lorraine, heading the French delegation, played a leading role. The French had opposed the Council for political reasons, but the spread of Calvinism in France later "revolutionized" their view. Ignatius Loyola did not attend, though several Jesuits, notably Diego Laynez, were important participants. The Council was plagued by politics from beginning to end (as was its convocation earlier), the fortunes of Habsburg–Valois rivalry and war frequently determining its continuation and course. Nevertheless it met and grappled with a good many of the most pressing questions of doctrine and reform, and it produced a large body of teaching and disciplinary legislation promulgated by Pope Pius IV in 1564 as its canons and decrees.[54]

Theoretically the Council had three main goals: (a) to effect needed reform in the Church, (b) to clarify and define disputed doctrine and condemn heresy, and (c) to restore the peace and unity of the Church. These aims were closely related and can be viewed, as they are in Cardinal Pole's keynote address at the second session in January 1546, as an attempt to remedy the ills and afflictions of the Church and to rebuild it. "We, the shepherds," he told the assembled Fathers, "should hold ourselves responsible for all the evils now burdening the flock of Christ," and he urged them in his remarkable plea for contrition to lead the Church to a genuine renewal and to peace. "It was an expression of the deepest sense of responsibility," says Jedin.[55] The Council, however, made little headway toward the goal of unity and peace. Religious division between Protestant and Catholic was now too deep-seated and entrenched to permit resolution in such a tribunal. Political reasons as well as doctrinal issues account for this, but most important were the rival conceptions of the Church that now prevailed. Whatever authority the Council claimed was rejected by the Protestants, who refused to cooperate with it, and this opposition stemmed now from very divergent views of the nature of the Church and of authority within it. The Council thus was confined in jurisdiction as well as in representation to the Catholic world, and it functioned not as an instrument of reconciliation or reunion but as a body defining and legislating for those who remained in the Catholic fold. It undertook this task from the start, agreeing after some initial argument to take up questions of doctrine and problems of reform simultaneously.

One of the earliest and most important of its doctrinal discussions was the long debate on justification. It went on for several months in 1546 and featured an extensive exchange on the notion of "double justification," a formulation of which Contarini had advanced at the Ratisbon conference. The Augustinian General Seripando defended it at Trent and found the young Jesuit Laynez in sharp disagreement. A detailed decree on this fundamental issue was finally worked out and was unanimously accepted by the Council at its sixth session in January 1547.[56] It declared that man is justified and saved only through God's grace freely bestowed on those who are baptized and have faith, but it insisted that man participates in the process through a disposition for grace and a voluntary reception of it. Justification, it declared, is also "the sanctification and renewal of the inward man," and it stressed the need for good works and observance of God's commandments if man is to grow in sanctity and gain eternal life. The Lutheran tenet of justification by faith alone as well as the concept of "double justification" were rejected, but the primacy of divine grace merited for man by Christ's redemptive act was acknowledged from beginning to end. The decree is completely scriptural in its argument and presentation and is not a scholastic formulation. This may in general be said of all the Tridentine decrees. Appended to the decree was a list of thirty-three short canons condemning specific "errors" concerning justification, both those deemed Pelagian and those clearly of Lutheran origin. It is often said that this decree and its canons—or, more broadly, the Tridentine pronouncements as a whole—shut the door on compromise and conciliation with the Protestants. By this time, however, the door was no longer ajar, and it can hardly be surprising that the Catholic Church, in view of the widespread doctrinal controversy that the Protestant Reformation had provoked, examined the basic theological issues and clarified its thought and faith. Not to have done so in these circumstances would have been to disavow that *magisterium* or teaching authority it claimed to exercise.

Other decrees and canons dealt with such doctrinal matters as the validity of both Holy Scripture and tradition as the twofold source of religious truth, the seven sacraments and the Mass, the existence of purgatory, and the invocation of the saints. The decree on Scripture and tradition was the first to be adopted by the Council, at its fourth session in April 1546, and was a sharp rejection of the "Scripture alone" principle of the Protestants. The decree on the Sacrifice of the Mass was approved at the twenty-second session in September 1562, and it ranks with the decree on justification as one of the two most important theological definitions of the Council. The Protestants had rejected the Mass as an "abomination" and "idolatry," and its abolition marked the decisive break with the old Church. The Council now affirmed and explained its sacrificial character.[57] It defined the Mass as a com-

memoration of the sacrifice of Christ on Calvary but also as a representation or rendering present of that unique sacrificial act.

Another major issue vigorously raised by the Protestants, the
primacy and authority of the pope in the Church, was not
formally discussed at the Council, though it was affirmed *de facto*
throughout the conciliar proceedings. The omission nevertheless
is extremely interesting. The Protestant point of view found no
supporters among the Fathers or theologians at Trent, but the
question of papal power was too sensitive and controversial,
impinging as it did on issues involving episcopal, conciliar, and
political authority, for the Council to reach agreement on a
detailed statement. The bypassing of the question is understanda-
ble, though paradoxical in view of the enhanced role of the pope
in the post-Tridentine Church. Stronger papal leadership and
executive power emerged not so much from the Council itself,
and certainly not from any of its declarations, as from the needs
and demands of the times. Evennett sees this development in
Catholicism as parallel to the secular development of stronger
monarchies in post-medieval Europe and "due to the same kind
of causes, necessities and conditions."[58]

In the area of reform the Council tackled four basic problems:
the training of priests, the duty of preaching the Gospel, the
jurisdiction of bishops, and the obligation of residence for bishops
and pastors. All four bear directly on the Church's pastoral
mission, that supreme task—*salus animarum suprema lex*—which is
indeed its raison d'être and by which its value and effectiveness
must be judged. These problems were raised and discussed in the
Council's early months and were the subject of several reform
decrees in 1546–1547, notably one establishing lectureships on
Scripture in cathedral churches and another imposing the obligation of preaching on bishops and pastors. However, it was not
until the final period of Trent that detailed and adequate legislation
pertaining to these matters was approved, and this came only after
a very serious deadlock and crisis in the Council over the nature
of the bishop's obligation to reside in his diocese had been
resolved.

The Council was split in 1562–1563 between those, led by the
archbishop of Granada and later the Cardinal of Lorraine, who
held insistently that the obligation of residence was a divine law,

a *ius divinum*, and those, led by Cardinal Simonetta and several
Italian bishops, who saw a threat to the papacy and curial tradition
in this line of reasoning. Behind the bitter and prolonged argument that developed lay the conviction, on the one hand, that the
divine law principle was essential if meaningful reform was to be
achieved and the fear, on the other, that such a principle overex-
tended the independence of the bishop and jeopardized the authority of the pope. The issue tended to divide the Spanish and French
Fathers from the Italian and the more radical reformers from the
more conservative. It threatened to break up the Council. This
dispute, which was carried on in an atmosphere of mutual suspicion and mistrust, was finally settled largely through the diplo-
macy of the presiding papal legate, Cardinal Giovanni Morone,
who in mid-1563 won the support of both factions for a compromise program. Jedin calls Morone the savior of the Council.[59] A
most skillful diplomat and a zealous reformer, he is the man
primarily responsible for Tridentine reform. After a standstill of
nearly a year, the Council moved again, and in its three concluding sessions—twenty-three, twenty-four, and twenty-five—the
Fathers approved several important reform decrees.[60]

These decrees are the chief contribution of the Council of Trent
to Catholic reform. They focus mainly, though not exclusively,
on the role and responsibility of the bishop. The Council's efforts,
Evennett tells us, "centered round the restoration of the episcopate, morally and administratively; and the strengthening of the
episcopate in every respect, as the nodal point of every aspect of
reform, may be regarded as a corner-stone of the counter-reformation Church."[61] The proposed and bitterly contested divine-
law sanction for episcopal residence was dropped, but the obligation of the bishop to reside in his see was vigorously affirmed.
The bishop's powers were considerably strengthened and en-
larged. He was given greater authority over clergy and members
of religious orders in his diocese with respect to exemptions and
papal dispensations as well as in matters of priestly conduct and
pastoral care. He was to hold a diocesan synod every year and
conduct a visitation of his diocese every two years. Provincial
synods were to be held every three years. The accumulation of
benefices, which was one of the worst abuses in the Church's
administrative structure, was forbidden, although this practice

was long in dying out. Trent's reforms were not as far-reaching as those proposed in the *Libellus* of Giustiniani and Quirini or in the *Consilium de emendanda ecclesia*, but the obligations and authority of the bishop were now more clearly defined and his primary role as pastor and teacher of his flock was forcefully emphasized.

Such was the core of Tridentine reform, though the Council's actions were not limited simply to restoring the episcopate; and of course the effects of that restoration were intended to reach far beyond the episcopal office. In this regard one reform deserves special mention. In the crucial decree of the twenty-third session in July 1563, which finally ended the deadlock over the *ius divinum*, the Council enjoined each bishop to establish a college or seminary for the education and training of future priests for his diocese, remedying thereby one of the most serious deficiencies in the late medieval Church. This innovation was directly inspired by Cardinal Reginald Pole's similar reform at the London synod in 1556 after he had returned to England as papal legate during the reign of Mary Tudor. The examples of Giberti in Verona and of the numerous Jesuit colleges springing up throughout Europe were also influential. This was a measure of truly historic importance, and Jedin declares that "it would not be an exaggeration to say that, if the Council of Trent had done nothing else for the renewal of the Church but initiate the setting up of diocesan seminaries for priests, it would have done a great deal."[62]

Judgment on the Council of Trent and its work is not a simple matter, and quite divergent analyses and appraisals have been made.[63] These often stem from one's initial preconceptions and assumptions, but the problem itself is enormous. The scope of the Council, the issues it dealt with, its political setting, the many personalities involved indicate the dimensions of the task. The pressures that affected it as well as the possibilities open to it also have to be borne in mind and realistically appraised. I think it fair to say that Trent must be judged in terms of the survival and renewal of the Catholic faith in these complicated and agitated times. Neither the schism itself nor its continuation can properly be attributed to it.[64] Whether the Council might have played a more conciliatory or ecumenical role does not seem under the circumstances a very practical question to pose. What then can be said about this General Council? It clarified and defined many doctrines then in dispute, it legislated some basic reforms, it rallied and strengthened the Catholic Church in the severe crisis it faced in the sixteenth century. It did not work a revolution in the ecclesiastical order or rid it of all the abuses that encumbered it, but it did affirm what it believed to be the truths of faith on a number of important points, and it took steps against some of the most salient defects and deficiencies in the Catholic Church. In this sense the Council can be said to have renewed and restructured the Catholic Church for the days ahead. If it was doctrinally speaking "the Church's answer to the Protestant Reformation," it was also the institutionalization of a significant program of ecclesiastical reform. The character and scope of both these achievements should not be underestimated. Despite all obstacles Trent accomplished much that was constructive, and under its sign a resurgent Church, still *mater et magistra* for a large portion of mankind, pursued its historic mission.

The conciliar decisions, of course, had to be implemented and enforced if they were to have real effect.[65] This takes us into the post-Tridentine era and beyond the limits of the account I set out to give. The impact of Trent—its interpretation, reception, and implementation—is unquestionably of great relevance and importance in the continuing story of Catholic reform, but this phase, like other important facets of the Catholic revival in the later sixteenth and seventeenth centuries and beyond—the history of the Jesuits, for example—has to await another volume. It is too complex and of too long a duration to lend itself to a summary treatment. I can, however, conclude this part of my essay with a few words about the immediate aftermath of the Council and the carrying out of its decrees.

In 1564 Pope Pius IV promptly approved and published the Tridentine decrees, circulated them to all Catholic bishops, and established a committee of eight cardinals, which later became the Congregation of the Council, to supervise their interpretation and oversee their enactment. That same year, pursuant to the Council's instructions, he issued a Tridentine Profession of Faith and published a revised Index of Forbidden Books that modified the excessive severity of an Index Paul IV had drawn up in 1559. His successor, Pius V, also completing work projected by the Council, produced the Roman Catechism in 1566, the revised Roman

Breviary in 1568, and a uniform Roman Missal in 1570. Due to a number of factors—old habits and practices, inertia, greed, political obstruction—the reform decrees of Trent were poorly and only very slowly implemented. There were many good bishops who now exemplified the Tridentine ideal—of whom Carlo Borromeo, the cardinal nephew of Pius IV and archbishop of Milan, and his friend and contemporary Gabriele Paleotti, the bishop (later archbishop) of Bologna, are outstanding[66]—but non-residence, plural holdings, and other abuses were still too prevalent. The Jesuit Cardinal Bellarmine frequently complained in the early seventeenth century of this failure to execute the Tridentine reforms and in a message to Paul V wrote that the reform of the Church, which is always necessary, could easily be achieved " 'if the Council of Trent were diligently observed.' "[67] The period after 1563, however, saw strong papal leadership exerted in that cause, and the situation did greatly improve. Delumeau declares that it improved "almost beyond belief."[68] There are many reasons for this transformation, gradual in some respects, sudden and swift in others, but the Council of Trent undeniably played a fundamental and essential role.

Certain basic lineaments stand out in this movement of Catholic reform from the days of Ximenes and Savonarola to the close of the Council of Trent. The first and most obvious was the widespread awareness of the need for reform and the many efforts made to achieve it. Yet initially the movement was scattered and disparate, a matter of individual initiative and endeavor rather than a coordinated program affecting the Church at large. Cardinal Ximenes is the major example of an ecclesiastical or institutional reformer in the early period. Erasmus and other Christian humanists, however widespread and deep their influence, worked in a private capacity, so to speak, and sought essentially personal enlightenment and reform, though indeed they envisioned the broader renewal of Christian life and society as a result. With the pontificate of Paul III the papacy at last began to exert an indispensable leadership, and Catholic reform became more concerted and official. It began to extend to the entire Church now in a serious state of crisis. The arrival of Contarini in Rome in 1535 ushered in this new era. New blood was infused into the papal administration, the Jesuits were organized and began their extensive activities, the General Council was finally convened at Trent. Despite its diversity the movement had an inner unity and coherence, and despite the difficulties that beset it it may be said to have followed an identifiable and progressive course.

In what did this inner unity and coherence consist? It was manifested in the first place in the desire for religious reform so emphatically expressed in the activities of the many individuals I have discussed. It is the dominant theme, the integrating principle, from Savonarola and Ximenes to Pius IV and Borromeo. I can include Luther, Zwingli, and Calvin and many others, of course, under such a rubric, and indeed one must in any comprehensive perspective on sixteenth-century reform. Evennett's, as well as Delumeau's, conception of two parallel Reformations comes to mind. But my focus is on Catholic reform and by definition limited to reformers who remained in the traditional Catholic Church and sought reform and renewal within the general framework of its teaching and authority. Aside from this, what features distinguish these Catholic reformers and link them in a common endeavor? As I see it, two characteristics run like a double rhythm through the Catholic Reformation: (a) the preoccupation of the Catholic reformers with the reform of the individual, and (b) their concern for the restoration and renewal of the Church's pastoral mission. Catholic reform, in short, had a marked personal and pastoral orientation.

Our reformers focused on the individual Christian and his moral and spiritual life. They sought essentially a *reformatio in membris* rather than dogmatic or structural change. The members of Christ's Church must lead better Christian lives and be instructed and guided along that path. This is the burden of Savonarola's prophetic preaching, the goal of Erasmus and other Christian humanists, the objective of Ignatius Loyola and his *Spiritual Exercises*. The Theatines, Capuchins, and Jesuits emphasized this in terms of the greater commitment and sanctification of their members. The reforms of Ximenes in Spain, of Giberti in Verona, and of the Council of Trent for the universal Church had this as the underlying purpose in their concern for the instruction and spiritual advancement of the faithful. "Man must be changed by religion, not religion by man" declared Egidio da Viterbo at the Fifth Lateran Council in 1512,[69] a dictum that in Pastor's judgment sums up "the theory of true Catholic reformation."[70] Even the doctrinal decrees of Trent, such as the very important one on justification, reflect this emphasis on the moral life of the Christian.

Such a focus presupposes concern for the reform of the institutional Church as well, for if men are to be changed by religion, then religion itself must be correctly represented and faithfully imparted. That reasoning lies behind Erasmus' insistence on the need to reform theology and to return to Holy Scripture and the Fathers. And it explains why the Church's pastoral mission—the work of teaching, guiding, and sanctifying its members—must be given primacy and rendered effective. Thus it follows that good men must be selected as bishops and must reside in their dioceses, that priests must be trained, that the Gospel must be preached and the young instructed, that venality and other abuses must be rooted out in the service of Christ and the salvation of souls. The Bark of Peter was not to be scuttled or rebuilt but to be steered back to its original course with the crew at their posts and responsive to their tasks. The state of the clergy loomed large in Catholic reform. If their ignorance, corruption, or neglect had been responsible for the troubles that befell the Church, as nearly everyone affirmed, then their reform required urgent attention and was the foundation and root of all renewal. This involved personal reform, that of the priests and prelates who are the instruments of the Church's mission and the ones principally charged with the *cura animarum*. The reform of the faithful would follow as the consequence, but the immediate objective was institutional or pastoral. The Church itself had to be revitalized and restored so that its true apostolate might be realized.

Obviously, personal reform and the renewal of the Church's pastoral mission were complementary goals—two sides of a single coin—but they also contained elements of tension and divergence. And different circumstances gave rise to different priorities and modes of action. Erasmus' approach was not the same as Giberti's; nor did the Jesuit apostle Peter Canisius operate in the same way as the archbishop of Milan Carlo Borromeo. Such differences were mainly functional perhaps, but behind the office or role of the individual reformer there were certainly dissimilarities in temperament and perspective. The contrast between Contarini and Carafa—one, the man of dialogue with the Protestants; the other, the man of the Inquisition—has often been underscored to bear this out. In this case, however, it seems more a matter of dealing with the Protestants than of reform per se, for both men were the principal authors of the *Consilium de emendanda ecclesia*. There was diversity, nevertheless, among the Catholic reformers, and in so broad a movement in so troubled a time it was bound to exist. That diversity in part involves the distinction and sometimes the tension between the reform of the Christian and the reform of the Church, though the movement as a whole had a basic and a common end. It sought the revival of religion, that is, the reform of the individual Christian in a Church renewed and rededicated to its spiritual tasks.

NOTES

1. It has been reprinted in Febvre's *Au coeur religieux du xvie siècle* (Paris: Sevpen, 1957), and there is an English translation in his *A New Kind of History*, ed. Peter Burke (London: Routledge & Kegan Paul, 1973), pp. 27–43. Dermot Fenlon sharply critiques the essay in "*Encore une question*: Lucien Febvre, the Reformation, and the School of *Annales*," *Historical Studies*, 9 (1956), 65–81.

2. *The Age of Reform, 1250–1550* (New Haven: Yale University Press, 1980), pp. 208–11, in particular.

3. *The Spirit of the Counter-Reformation*, ed. John Bossy (Cambridge: Cambridge University Press, 1968), I shall refer to this work hereafter as Evennett.

4. Ibid., p. 7.

5. (London: Burns & Oates; Philadelphia: Westminster, 1977), pp. 160–61 in particular. Another book of Delumeau's, *Le Christianisme va-t-il mourir?* (Paris: Hachette, 1978), also presents his view of the history of the Church and of the two Reformations and relates his overall perspective to the situation of Christianity today. See also Wolfgang Reinhard's "Reformation, Counter-Reformation, and the Early Modern State: A Reassessment," *The Catholic Historical Review*, 75 (1989), 383–404, which views the Reformation and Counter-Reformation as two "almost parallel" processes.

6. *The Foundations of Early Modern Europe, 1460–1559* (New York:

Norton, 1970), p. x. This work is an excellent brief introduction to this "period of rapid, comprehensive change."

7. The sermon (as well as other information relating to Savonarola) is in John C. Olin, *The Catholic Reformation: Savonarola to Ignatius Loyola* (New York: Harper & Row, 1969), chap. 1. This work hereafter will be referred to as CR.

8. The first chapter of Bataillon's *Erasme et l'Espagne: Recherches sur l'histoire spirituelle du xvie siècle* (Paris: Droz, 1937) is devoted to Ximenes' reforms.

9. Basil Hall, "The Trillingual College of San Ildefonso and the Making of the Complutensian Polyglot Bible," in *Studies in Church History. V. The Church and Academic Learning*, ed. G. J. Cuming (Leiden: Brill, 1969), pp. 114–46. See also Otis H. Green, *Spain and the Western Tradition* III (Madison: University of Wisconsin Press, 1965), pp. 16–19 and passim; and Jerry H. Bentley, *Humanists and Holy Writ* (Princeton: Princeton University Press, 1983), chap. 3.

10. The thesis that holds that Catholic reform and revival began in earnest prior to the Lutheran revolt and originated in the Spain of Cardinal Ximenes was first advanced by Wilhelm Maurenbrecher in his *Geschichte der katholischen Reformation* (Nordlingen: Beck, 1880), a work that pioneered the concept of an independent Catholic Reformation predating Protestantism. See the comments regarding this "thesis" in Evennett, pp. 11–13.

11. Charles Trinkaus, *In Our Image and Likeness: Humanity and Divinity in Italian Humanist Thought*, 2 vols. (Chicago: The University of Chicago Press, 1970), stresses the religious orientation of Italian humanism and views the movement essentially as a search for a more relevant secular–Christian theological synthesis. On more specific themes, see Charles Stinger's *Humanism and the Church Fathers* (Albany: State University of New York Press, 1977) and Bentley's *Humanists and Holy Writ*.

12. See Erasmus' Ep. 108, addressed to Colet, in *The Correspondence of Erasmus* I, trans. R. A. B. Mynors (Toronto: University of Toronto Press, 1974), pp. 202–206. Erasmus also wrote a short sketch of Colet's life in a letter to Jodocus Jonas in 1521; see *Christian Humanism and the Reformation: Selected Writings of Erasmus*, ed. John C. Olin, 3rd ed. (New York: Fordham University Press, 1987), chap. 9. This edition will be referred to hereafter as CHR[3]. See CR, chap. 3, for further references to Colet. This latter chapter also presents Colet's Convocation Sermon of 1512 on the reformation of the clergy.

13. For a brief introduction to Erasmus and his work see CHR[3]. The volume is prefaced by a biographical sketch. See also John C. Olin, *Six Essays on Erasmus* (New York: Fordham University Press, 1979). CR, chap. 6, contains Erasmus' adage-essay *Sileni Alcibiadis*.

14. Ep. 1891, in *Opus epistolarum Des. Erasmi Roterodami*, edd. P. S. Allen, H. M. Allen, and H. W. Garrod, 12 vols. (Oxford: Clarendon, 1906–1958), VII, 11. 183–95.

15. See CR, chap. 8, and Eugene F. Rice, Jr., "The Humanist Idea of Christian Antiquity: Lefèvre d'Etaples and His Circle," *Studies in the Renaissance*, 9 (1962), 126–41.

16. In this context of reform I cannot fail to mention More's great book *Utopia*, which was first published in 1516. It is primarily a social critique, and it expresses values and ideals shared by Erasmus and other humanists.

17. See, for example, Henri de Lubac, s.j., *Exégèse médiévale* (Paris: Aubier, 1964), Second Part, II, chap. 10.

18. This statement of Adrian VI's is part of his instruction to the papal nuncio Chieregati at the Diet of Nuremberg and is in CR, chap. 9.

19. See below, p. 28.

20. See H. Outram Evennett, "The New Orders," in *The New Cambridge Modern History. II. The Reformation, 1520–1559*, ed. G. R. Elton (Cambridge: Cambridge University Press, 1962), chap. 9. I should note too that reforms were also taking place in the older monastic and mendicant orders in the late fifteenth and early sixteenth centuries. Cardinal Ximenes' reform of the Franciscans in Castile (see above, p. 5) and Gregorio Cortese's reform of the Italian Benedictines (see below, p. 18) are two notable examples.

21. Evennett, p. 36. This paragraph in my essay is practically a summation of Evennett's central theme.

22. See CR, chap. 2, for the charter of the Oratory and further bibliographical information.

23. Ludwig Pastor especially in his *The History of the Popes from the Close of the Middle Ages*, trans. F. I. Antrobus, R. F. Kerr, et al., 40 vols. (St. Louis: B. Herder, 1891–1953), x 388ff., stresses the importance of this event. This work hereafter will be referred to as Pastor.

24. On the Theatines and their rule see CR, chap. 10.

25. The original Italian text of Carafa's *informazione* is in *Concilium Tridentinum: Diariorum, actorum, epistolarum, tractatuum nova collectio*, edd. S. Merkle et al., 13 vols. (Freiburg: Görresgesellschaft, 1901–1938), xii 67–77. There is an English version in *Reform Thought in Sixteenth-Century Italy*, ed. Elisabeth G. Gleason (Chico, Calif.: Scholars Press, 1981), pp. 55–80.

26. See CR, chap. 12, which also contains the Capuchin constitutions of 1536.

27. Edward Peters, *Inquisition* (New York: Free Press, 1988; repr. Berkeley: University of California Press, 1989), pp. 107ff. Peters' book

is a comprehensive survey of the various inquisitions as well as of what he calls "the myth of *The Inquisition*."

28. Cf. the comments on this "turning point" in Dermot Fenlon, *Heresy and Obedience in Tridentine Italy: Cardinal Pole and the Counter Reformation* (Cambridge: Cambridge University Press, 1972), pp. 22–23, 51–53.

29. See CR, chap. 11, for some of Giberti's diocesan reforms.

30. A major part of Contarini's treatise *De officio episcopi* is in CR, chap. 7, where there is bibliographical information relating to Contarini. Two further references must be mentioned: Felix Gilbert, "Religion and Politics in the Thought of Gasparo Contarini," in *Action and Conviction in Early Modern Europe*, edd. Theodore K. Rabb and Jerrold E. Seigel (Princeton: Princeton University Press, 1969), pp. 90–116, and J. B. Ross, "Gasparo Contarini and His Friends," *Studies in the Renaissance*, 17 (1970), 192–232.

31. On this question see Nelson H. Minnich and Elisabeth G. Gleason, "Vocational Choices: An Unknown Letter of Pietro Querini to Gasparo Contarini and Niccolò Tiepolo (April, 1512)," *The Catholic Historical Review*, 75 (1989), 1–20.

32. "Religion and Politics in the Thought of Gasparo Contarini," pp. 114–15.

33. The text of the *Libellus* is in *Annales Camaldulenses*, edd. J. B. Mittarelli and A. Costadoni, 9 vols. (Venice, 1755–1773), ix 612–719. The longest section, cols. 668–714, focuses on reform. See also Hubert Jedin, *A History of the Council of Trent* I–II, trans. Dom Ernest Graf, O.S.B. (St. Louis: B. Herder, 1957, 1961), i 128–30. This work will hereafter be referred to as Jedin.

34. On the Fifth Lateran Council, which met in Rome from May 1512 to March 1517, see CR, chaps. 4 and 5. It was originally called by Pope Julius II, but Leo X continued it. Especially notable is the opening address in 1512 by the Augustinian General Egidio da Viterbo (Giles of Viterbo). Its keynote is the need for reform and the role of the Council as the essential means to attain it. This important address is in the document section of this volume.

35. See Francesco C. Cesareo's *Humanism and Catholic Reform: The Life and Work of Gregorio Cortese, 1483–1548* (Bern: Lang, 1990).

36. Wilhelm Schenk, *Reginald Pole, Cardinal of England* (London: Longmans, 1950) gives an excellent picture of Pole in this Catholic reform milieu. See also Fenlon, *Heresy and Obedience*.

37. The fullest account is in Pastor, XI–XII.

38. The awesome figure of Christ as Judge is the dynamic center of

this huge fresco. Michelangelo's composition depicts an eschatological theme—the *adventus Domini* of Matt. 24:30–31—but there could hardly be a more dramatic representation in the very heart of Christendom of the great crisis that had come. On the painting see Charles de Tolnay, *Michelangelo. V. The Final Period* (Princeton: Princeton University Press, 1971), pp. 19–50, as well as the comments of Ernest Gordon Rupp in *Luther's Progress to the Diet of Worms* (New York: Harper & Row, 1964), pp. 48–49.

39. Jedin, I 419. See also Jedin's appraisal of Paul III in ibid., 288–90, 444–45.

40. See *A Reformation Debate: Sadoleto's Letter to the Genevans and Calvin's Reply*, ed. John C. Olin (New York: Harper & Row, 1966).

41. The *Consilium* is in CR, chap. 3, and is reprinted in this volume. For comment see also Jedin, I 423ff.

42. Jedin, I 377ff. See also Peter Matheson, *Cardinal Contarini at Regensburg* (Oxford: Clarendon, 1972).

43. See Peter A. Quinn, "Ignatius Loyola and Gian Pietro Carafa: Catholic Reformers at Odds," *The Catholic Historical Review*, 67 (1981), 386–400.

44. The account that follows is supplemented by the study in the Appendix of this volume: "The Idea of Pilgrimage in the Experience of Ignatius Loyola." See also *The Autobiography of St. Ignatius Loyola*, ed. John C. Olin, trans. Joseph F. O'Callaghan (New York: Harper & Row, 1974); John C. Olin, "Erasmus and St. Ignatius Loyola," *Six Essays on Erasmus*, pp. 75–92; and CR, chap. 14. I would also like to call attention to two issues of *Studies in the Spirituality of Jesuits* (published at The Institute of Jesuit Sources in St. Louis): John W. O'Malley, S.J., "The Jesuits, St. Ignatius, and the Counter Reformation: Some Recent Studies and Their Implications for Today," 14, No. 1 (January 1982), 1–28; and Philip Endean, S.J., "Who Do You Say Ignatius Is? Jesuit Fundamentalism and Beyond," 19, No. 5 (November 1987), 1–53. Evennett's main focus, chaps. 3 and 4, is on Ignatius and the Jesuits as the chief agents of Catholic renewal (p. 43), "the richest amalgams" of a broad spectrum of influence (p. 62). Note also the two documents in this volume relating to the formation of the Society of Jesus.

45. The best English edition of the *Spiritual Exercises* is that of Louis J. Puhl, S.J. (Westminster, Md.: Newman, 1951). The *Exercises* is very well analyzed in its historical context in Evennett, chap. 3. See also the article on Ignatius appended to this volume.

46. The statement or First Sketch of the Society of Jesus is in the document section of this volume.

47. Jedin, I 439.

48. See the Letter to Diego de Gouvea in the document section below.

49. Evennett, p. 75.

50. For a substantial and comprehensive history of the order, see William V. Bangert, s.j., *A History of the Society of Jesus* (St. Louis: The Institute of Jesuit Sources, 1972).

51. Jedin, I 192–96. Hubert Jedin's *History of the Council of Trent* is the surest guide to the history of the Council and its background (four volumes in German, the first two of which have been translated into English). Volume I covers a wide range of religious and Church history in the fifteenth and early sixteenth centuries; Volume II deals with the first session at Trent, 1545–1547. Jedin also has a brief study of the final period at Trent, 1562–1563, entitled in English translation *Crisis and Closure of the Council of Trent: A Retrospective View from the Second Vatican Council*, trans. N. D. Smith (London: Sheed & Ward, 1967). For a short survey, see his article, "Trent, Council of," in *The New Catholic Encyclopedia*, XIV.

52. On Cervini, who had a very short reign as Pope Marcellus II in 1555, and his views concerning the papacy, reform, and related issues, see William V. Hudon, "Papal, Episcopal, and Secular Authority in the Work of Marcello Cervini," *Cristianesimo nella storia*, 9 (1988), 493–521.

53. See illustration of the published safe-conduct. Pius IV's efforts to have Protestant representatives attend when the Council reconvened in 1562 came to nought.

54. *Canons and Decrees of the Council of Trent*, trans. H. J. Schroeder, o.p. (St. Louis: B. Herder, 1941). Hereafter referred to as Schroeder.

55. Jedin, II 25–26. See also Fenlon, *Heresy and Obedience*, pp. 119–20.

56. This decree and its accompanying canons are in *A Reformation Debate*, ed. Olin, Appendix II, and in Schroeder, pp. 29–46.

57. Schroeder, pp. 144–45.

58. Evennett, pp. 89–94.

59. See *Crisis and Closure*, chap. 6.

60. Schroeder, pp. 164–79, 190–213, 217–53. The reform decrees of the twenty-third and twenty-fourth sessions are reprinted in the document section of this volume.

61. Evennett, p. 97.

62. *Crisis and Closure*, p. 120.

63. Cf., for example, the two brief chapters on Trent in A. G. Dickens, *The Counter Reformation* (New York: Harcourt, Brace & World, 1969), chaps. 7 and 8, with the account here or with Evennett's comments or Jedin's. Ozment's *Age of Reform* devotes only a few pages to Trent, pp. 406–409 (out of 438).

64. See Robert E. McNally, s.j., "The Council of Trent and the German Protestants," *Theological Studies*, 25, No. 1 (March 1964), 1–22.

65. On this broad subject see Delumeau, *Catholicism Between Luther and Voltaire*, chap. 2, and Giuseppe Alberigo, "La 'reception' du Concile de Trente par l'Eglise catholique romaine," *Irénikon*, 58 (1985), 311–37.

66. See *San Carlo Borromeo: Catholic Reform and Ecclesiastical Politics in the Second Half of the Sixteenth Century*, edd. John M. Headley and John B. Tomaro (Washington, D.C.: Folger Books, 1988), especially Tomaro's "San Carlo Borromeo and the Implementation of the Council of Trent," pp. 67–84; and Paolo Prodi, "The Application of the Tridentine Decrees: The Organization of the Diocese of Bologna During the Episcopate of Cardinal Gabriele Paleotti," in *The Late Italian Renaissance*, ed. Eric Cochrane (New York: Harper & Row, 1970), pp. 226–43.

67. Quoted in Alberigo, "La 'reception' du Concile de Trente," 324.

68. *Catholicism Between Luther and Voltaire*, p. 33.

69. See note 34.

70. Pastor, VII 10.

CARDINAL XIMENES

THE COMPLUTENSIAN POLYGLOT

TITIAN, *The Council of Trent*

DECRETVM

PRIMVM PVBLICATVM IN
SECVNDA SESSIONE SACRI
Concilij Tridentini, *sub* Pio PP. IIII.
die 26. Februarij 1562.

FIDES PVBLICA, SEV SALVVS
conductus quem sacrosancta Synodus &c. Dat
omnibus & singulis Germanicæ nationis
sub ea forma quam alias ipsi petie-
runt, cuius Tenor est qui
subsequitur.

RIPAE.

M.D. LXII.

SAFE-CONDUCT

DOCUMENTS

The seven documents in this section, dating from 1512 to 1563, illustrate the desire for Church reform and efforts made to achieve it as well as other aspects of Catholic renewal and revival in this critical period. As contemporary sources they flesh out the narrative essay that precedes them. With the exception of Egidio da Viterbo's address to the Fifth Lateran Council—the first document—their occasion and context are discussed in the essay.

1

Egidio da Viterbo's Address to the Fifth Lateran Council May 3, 1512

The Fifth Lateran Council was called by Pope Julius II in the midst of his war with Louis XII of France and in opposition to a French-sponsored Council at Pisa. It opened in Rome on May 3, 1512, at the Lateran Basilica, and Egidio da Viterbo (Giles of Viterbo), General of the Augustinian Order and one of the most renowned scholars and preachers in Italy of his day, addressed the initial assembly. He spoke in the presence of the pope and nearly one hundred prelates who composed the Council, and his address is a dramatic appeal to those gathered before him to take action to reform the Church and remedy the ills that beset Christendom. The Council continued to meet until March 1517 and did enact some reform decrees, but unfortunately these measures as well as the moving appeal of Egidio had little effect.

Egidio's address is reprinted here from CR, chap. 4, where there is also additional bibliographical information. The Latin text is in G. M. Mansi, *Sacrorum conciliorum nova et amplissima collectio,* 53 vols. in 58 (Paris: Walter, 1901–1927), XXXII 669–76. For further comment, see John W. O'Malley, s.j., *Giles of Viterbo on Church and Reform* (Leiden: Brill, 1968). CR. chap. 5, has the Council's major reform decree, *Supernae dispositionis arbitrio.*

THERE IS NO ONE HERE, I believe, who does not wonder, when there are so many men in the city who are famed indeed for their ability to speak with dignity and eloquence, why I, who can in no way be compared with these brilliant men, should be the one to appear before us and should dare to speak on so important a matter and in so great an assembly that the world has none more esteemed or more sacred. I might indeed say that something has intervened, and for this reason I have been preferred over the others, not because of any excellence but because of earlier times and activities. And so for this reason I seem to have been invited as the first to cast a spear in this conflict and to begin the Holy Lateran Council.

For about twenty years ago, as much as I was able and my meager strength allowed, I explained the Gospels to the people, made known the predictions of the prophets, expounded to nearly all of Italy John's Apocalypse concerning the destiny of the Church, and repeatedly asserted that those who were then listening would see great agitation and destruction in the Church and would one day behold its correction.[1] Now it has seemed proper that he who had said these things would happen bears witness that they have happened, and he who had so often cried out "My eyes will see salutary times" now at last cries out "My eyes have seen the salutary and holy beginning of the awaited renewal." If only you be present, Renewer of the world, Child of a divine Father, Preserver and Savior of mortal men, you may grant to me the power to speak, to my address the power to persuade, to the Fathers the power to celebrate, not with words but with deeds, a true, holy, and full Council, to root out vice, to arouse virtue, to catch the foxes who in this season swarm to destroy the holy vineyard, and finally to call fallen religion back to its old purity, its ancient brilliance, its original splendor, and its own sources. Thus I shall say of a Council both how useful it is for the Church at all times and how necessary it is for our times, with the preface that I would not dare alter the prophetic writings, but would make use of the words and speeches in their entirety, as they are accustomed to be read, not only because men must be changed by religion, not religion by men, but because the language of truth is

---

[1] The time as well as the character of Egidio's prophetic praching coincide with Savonarola's. See Savonarola's Renovation sermon of January 13, 1495, in CR, chap. 1.

straightforward. And from the beginning this division came to mind: some things are divine, others celestial, others human.

Divine things certainly do not need correction because they are not subject to motion or change. But celestial and human things, being subject to movement, long for renewal. For when the moon has come into position with the sun and when the sun has descended from the summer solstice to the winter solstice to the great loss, as it were, of men, the loss is completely restored. Nature's law demands that the loss of light be made up for and that whatever was taken away on the wane be restored to men on the ascent. If the paths of the stars in the heavens, even though constant, eternal, and everlasting, nevertheless return and are restored, what then does this third division of things do, since they are changing, transitory, and mortal? Indeed, either they inevitably perish in a quick destruction, or they are restored in a continual renewal. For what food is for bodies that they may live, and procreation for species that they may be perpetuated, correction, cultivation, instruction serve as the occasion demands for human souls. And as no living things can long survive without nourishment from food, so man's soul and the Church cannot perform well without the attention of Councils. If you should take rain from the meadows, streams from the gardens, tilling from the fields, pruning from the vines, and nourishment from living beings, these would soon dry up and grow wild, and the latter would cease living and die. Such was the case after the time of Constantine when, though much splendor and embellishment were added to religion, the austerity of morals and living was greatly weakened.

As often as the holding of Councils was delayed, we saw the divine Bride forsaken by her Spouse and that message of the Gospel accomplished which was recited yesterday: "A little while and you shall not see me." We saw Christ sleeping in a small boat, we saw the force of the winds, the fury of the heretics, raging against the bright sails of truth. We saw evil's desperate recklessness battering the laws, authority, and majesty of the Church. We saw wicked greed, the cursed thirsting for gold and possessions. We saw, I say, violence, pillage, adultery, incest—in short, the scourge of every crime—so confound all that is sacred and profane, and so attack the holy bark, that this bark has been almost swamped by the waves of sin and nearly engulfed and destroyed.

Once again at the prompting of that Spirit to whom public prayers have this day been decreed, the Fathers have had recourse to a Council. As quickly as possible they have corrected and settled all matters. They have exercised their command over the winds and storms, and as though carried to the safest of ports they have compelled might to yield to reason, injustice to justice, vice to virtue, storms and waves to serenity and tranquillity. And they have sung a hymn to the Holy Spirit, to the God of fishermen, of the sea, and of waters: "Deep waters cannot quench love," and "The winter is past, the rains are over and gone. . . . Arise, my beloved" [Cant. 8:7, 2:11–13]. For the Bride lies still, as the leaves of the trees in winter, but with the effort of Councils does she arise and grow strong, as the trees bring forth their leaves in the springtime when the sun returns. With the rays of the returning sun the favoring west wind blows, and the young trees bloom forth in their richness; so with the light of Councils and the Holy Spirit the winds blow and the dead eyes of the Church come to life again and receive the light. And here the other part of the prophecy is fulfilled: "Again a little while and you shall see me." Therefore, she wishes nothing for herself except that the Holy Spirit's light which is extinguished without Councils, like a new fire struck from flint, be again kindled and recovered in the Councils. Paul, the glory of the Apostles, when he declared the source of salvation, said: "Without faith we cannot please God." But without Councils, faith cannot stand firm. Without Councils, therefore, we cannot be saved.

In order to prove from experience what we assert as true by reason, we must consider that there are three fundamental articles of belief from which flows the Church's entire faith. The first is the unity of the divine nature. The second is the most blessed Trinity of parent, child, and love in the same nature. The third is the conception of the divine Child in the womb of the Virgin. On these, as on the highest peaks and most sacred mountains, the remaining nine parts of faith and all piety are founded. "His foundation upon the holy mountains [the Lord loves]." Truly, unity is called the mountain of God because God's essence and nature consist precisely in unity. And in order that we may reflect upon the fact that this unity is not solitary and sterile, but rather endowed with the richest abundance, fertile mountain is added. And when indeed the Word is given body in the Virgin, the prophet describes the mountain as coagulated.[2]

Thus threefold is this vineyard situated on the mountaintops, a vineyard which prophecies have said would be and the Gospels have revealed is here. But now the vineyard had perished, for, as David testified, a wild beast from the woods had ravaged it, that is, the ferment of philosophy had laid it waste. First Arius, who shattered the doctrine of unity, tried to tear down the mountain. Next came Sabellius, who confused the Persons [of the Trinity]. The third was Photius, who overthrew the Virgin Birth with impure recklessness. Like three most base giants, seduced by the desire for glory and the longing for change, they dared to move the mountains from their place, so that they might open a way to attack and pull down heaven. And now their prayers were answered, for with arms the princes ordered accepted what these men by philosophy were persuading. Philosophy was pressing us with its arguments; arms with standards gathered attacked. The former by deceit, the latter by force, were trying to overthrow the faith. Philosophy tried to overturn what was believed; force strove to destroy those who believed. The first raged against pious souls; the second, against living bodies. What was the divine Bride, now on the very brink of destruction, to do in order to escape? Whose trust, whose strength, whose aid could she beseech? The tempest was raging, the boat was sinking. In short, so as not to delay on many points, no way to flee, no way to escape, was found save only the Council of Nicaea when God appeared to Silvester, who sat at the helm, a man already suffering shipwreck, and said: "O you of little faith, why have you doubted?" And immediately by divine power he restored the mountains of faith and destroyed the rash monsters. Whereby the Bride, having been rescued, learned from experience that when she saw any misfortune threatening

---

[2]The above references are to Ps. 86(87):1–2 ("His foundation . . ."), Is. 5:1 (for fertile mountain), and Ps. 67(68):16, in the Vulgate version (for the mountains as coagulated, that is, *mons coagulatus*). In the paragraph that follows in the text David's testimony and prayer concerning the vineyard refer to Ps. 79(80), the same psalm quoted in the papal bull *Exsurge, Domine*, condemning Luther in June 1520.

her she had no defense more effective than a Council, where alone
no waters extinguish the fire of charity in the Church and the
Holy Spirit makes a resting-place in our souls, even as, according
to the testimony of Moses, the only Conqueror of the waves and
Ruler of the storms is borne across the waters.

What I have just said about faith, which indeed would not exist
without the establishment of a Council, I wish applied to temper-
ance, justice, wisdom, and the other virtues. Certainly we all
desire idleness rather than hard work, leisure rather than activity,
pleasure rather than deprivation. But whenever we take notice of
what is done at Councils, so that an evaluation may be made, the
question of morals and living be investigated, and the wicked
discovered, judged, and punished, while, on the other hand, the
upright are attracted, encouraged, and praised, unbelievable incen-
tives to cultivate virtue are inspired, with the result that men take
courage, decide on the better course of action, undertake to give
up vice and pursue virtue, and strive after nothing that is not
honorable and lofty. It is this which has been the distinguishing
characteristic of a Council, from which shone forth, as though
from the Trojan horse, the brightest lights of so many minds.
This approval of virtue, this condemnation of vice brought forth
the Basils, Chrysostoms, Damascenes in Greece, the Jeromes,
Ambroses, Augustines, Gregorys in Italy. And what books, writings, and memorials, what a wealth of learning, instruction, and
divine wisdom have they not gathered into the Christian treasury?

Since time does not permit, I pass over what should hardly be
passed over, namely, the question of those in charge of the
churches and the shepherds of the people on whom certainly rest
the entire Christian faith and salvation. For just as this lower world
is ruled by the movement and light of heaven, so the Christian
peoples are governed by rulers as though by heavenly shepherds,
who, if they are to be good, must teach others while shining
themselves with the light of learning, and must lead the way by
their own actions, practicing the pious deeds they preach. These
are the two things that Christ, the Prince of shepherds, taught
when He ordered them to carry burning lamps in order to teach
clearly and to gird themselves in order to live piously [Luke 12:35].
At the same time He Himself did this in an extraordinary way,
being the Light of the world and the Wisdom of the Divine Father,

and He was called the Holy of Holies because He excelled all upright men in the holiness of His Life. And because of this He said "I am the Good Shepherd." The evangelist who writes that He began first to act, then to teach [Acts 1:1], testifies what He said on both these points. And indeed those twelve leaders who were established as princes over the entire earth were inspired and perfected by the power of the Spirit, and so comprehended the meaning of heaven that they merited the name of heaven, as the very well known prophecy proclaims: "The heavens declare the glory of God." By this we are warned that we should honor the fame of those leaders who imitated and followed the light of heaven by their wisdom and its order by their sanctity. History records how much attention therefore Councils have given to this matter, which is by far the most important of all. For those who join a holy rule of life to distinguished learning are sought out from every part of the earth by the Council's Fathers and are raised up and adorned with the highest praise of those selecting them, with the fruits of the churches, and with the favor, the joy, and the applause of the people.

What should I say about that most serious and most dangerous matter of all, which everyone in our days deplores? I mean the wrongs inflicted by princes, the insolence of armies, the threats of armed force. For what can be heard or thought of that is more pitiable than that the queen of heaven and earth, the Church, is forced to be a slave to might, to surrender, or to shudder before the weapons of plunderers? This pestilence today spreads so far, rises to such a height, and gathers so much strength that all the authority of the Church and its freedom conferred by God seem overturned, struck to the ground, and completely destroyed. Therefore, beware, O Julius II, Supreme Pontiff, beware lest you believe that any man has ever conceived a better or more beneficial plan than you have conceived at the prompting of the Holy Spirit in convening a Council, whose decrees certainly no kings, no princes can despise; nor can they disregard its commands or disparage its authority. For if there are some who by chance have dared to esteem lightly the pope alone, defenseless by himself, they have become accustomed to fear and respect him when he is provided, by the authority of a Council, with the support and devotion of princes and nations.

If we recall the accomplishments of Councils, we realize that there is nothing more effective, greater, or more powerful than these. It was at a Council that Gregory X designated Rudolph Emperor in opposition to John of Spain and Alphonso of Lusitania, at a Council that Martin IV took measures against Pedro of Aragon, at a Council that Boniface VIII decreed against King Philip. It was at a Council that once Gregory and then Eugenius, within the memory of the Fathers, joined the Greek church to the Latin.[3] It was at a Council that both Innocent IV and Gregory IX took action against the Emperor Frederick. Indeed in this very temple, the foremost of all, ever accustomed to conquer enemies and never to be conquered, it was only at a Council that Innocent II cast down his adversaries, that Alexander III triumphed over [the antipope] Victor and his allies, that Innocent III removed Otto from the Empire, and that Martin V routed the hostile forces of the tyrants. And lest I enumerate every case, whatever measure is worthy of praise, whatever deed is worthy of glory in the Church since the time of Melchiades, either in holding off an enemy or in reconciling a state, in each instance it has had its origin in Councils and therefore should be associated with them.

For what else is a holy Council if not an object of fear for the evil, a hope for the upright, a rejection of errors, a seed-bed and revival of virtues, whereby the deceit of the devil is conquered, the allurements of the senses removed, reason restored to its lost citadel, and justice returned from heaven to earth? Indeed God returns to men. For if He has said "Where two or three are gathered in my name, I come to them and am in the midst of them" [Matt. 18:20], with what greater joy does He join that gathering where not only two or three have come, but so many leaders of the Church? If John calls the shepherds of the churches angels, what is there that so great an assembly of angels cannot seek by its petitions or obtain by its prayers from God [Apoc. 1–3]? Here Eve is called back from exile; here the head of the serpent is crushed by the heel of a more holy maiden. Abraham is led forth from the land of the Chaldeans; Agar the slave-girl submits

---

[3] I.e., Gregory X at the Second Council of Lyons in 1274 and Eugenius IV at the Council of Florence in 1439. Egidio actually says *Gregorius alter*, but it was the same Gregory X mentioned above who sought to reunite the Greeks.

to her mistress. A covenant with God is again made, and a spiritual circumcision is introduced. Here the father of patriarchs makes firm a ladder and opens an entrance into heaven, and he wrestles with God and receives a name by seeing God. Here the people, as though oppressed by famine in the wilderness, obtain aid from God, receive the bread of heaven and of the angels, and feast at a delectable heavenly banquet. Here, although the hearts of men have turned to stone, as it were, struck by the rod of Moses, they pour forth streams of water. Here the treasure hidden in a field is dug up, the pearl is bought, the lamps are lighted, the seed is sown in good soil, the grain of mustard seed grows up into a tree, and the wild olive is grafted onto the bountiful olive tree. Oh, those blessed times that have brought forth Councils! How foolish are the times that have not recognized their importance! How unhappy those that have not allowed them!

Since we have spoken summarily of the past benefits from Councils, let us now, as briefly as possible, touch upon those from our Council. Therefore I call upon you, Julius II, Supreme Pontiff, and Almighty God calls upon you, that God who has wished you to act as His vicar on earth, who long ago chose you alone from so greate a senate, who has sustained you as bridegroom of His Church into the ninth year, who has given you a good mind for planning and a great facility for acting (to none of your predecessors has He ever given so much) so that you might drive away robbers, clear the highways, put an end to insurrections, and raise the most magnificent temple of the Lord ever seen by man, and so that you might do what no one before has been able to do, make the arms of the Church fearful to great kings that you might extend your rule and recover Rimini, Faenza, Ravenna, and many other places. Even though the enemy can seize these, he cannot prevent you as pope from accomplishing all this. For the excellence of great princes must be appraised not on the basis of chance or accident, but from plans and actions. Now two things remained for you to do, that you convene a Council and that you declare war on the common enemy of Christians. And what from the beginning you always intended, pledged, and proposed, may you now perform for God, for the Christian flock, and for your own piety and fidelity. Indeed, you should know that you have given great hope to all good men, inasmuch as you who had been forced to postpone these matters by the injustice of the wars and evil times could not be induced to neglect or renounce them by threats, force, or defeat. Indeed, your soul had been strengthened by that perseverance so that these waves, as numerous as they are, could not extinguish your strong love. And so God also who, besides all these immortal favors which I have mentioned to stir your soul, called you back to life in those earlier years at Bologna and then at Rome, when it was thought even within your own palace that you were dead, and preserved you to accomplish these great deeds, so that God Himself by the most evident miracle might restore life to a pope that had expired and the pope by a holy Council might restore life to the Church that had expired, and so that the Church, together with a reviving pope, might restore morals to life, this God, I say, entreats and orders you to consider these two things in your heart, to give attention to them, and to accomplish them. And just as He commands the prophet, He commands you to tear down, root up, and destroy errors, luxury, and vice, and to build, establish, and plant moderation, virtue, and holiness [Jer. 1:10].

Many things, but especially the loss of the army, should prompt us to perform these deeds, for indeed I think that it was an act of divine Providence that relying on arms alien to the Church we suffered defeat, so that returning to our own arms we might become victors.[4] But our weapons, to use the words of the Apostle, are piety, devotion, honesty, prayers, offerings, the shield of faith, and the arms of light [Eph. 6:13–17; Rom. 13:12]. If we return to these with the aid of the Council, just as with arms that were not ours we were inferior to an enemy, so with our own weapons we shall be superior to every enemy. Call to mind, I beg, the war that Moses waged against King Amalec [Ex. 17]. You will see that God's chosen people when trusting in the sword were always conquered, but when they offered prayers they were always victorious. Joshua led the army into battle; Aaron with Hur and Moses climbed the mountain. The former with their bodies armed engaged the enemy; the latter with hearts made clean prayed to God. Those strove with swords; these with prayers. Those fought

---

[4]Egidio refers, of course, to the defeat of the Spanish–papal forces by the French at Ravenna on Easter Sunday, April 11, 1512. See Pastor, VI 398–406.

with iron; these, with piety. We see both kinds of arms—of the
military and of religion—but with God instructing us let us now
learn which are ours. As long as Moses raised his hands, He says,
our army gained the mastery, but when he put his hands down
the army wavered. And lest we suspect that this happened by
chance, at the end of this account it is written that the hand of
God and the war is against Amalec, that is, against the enemy of
the Church from generation to generation. Certainly by these
words God warns that both the generation and the Church of
Moses and of Christ is conquered by military arms, but conquers
by zealous piety, and that by striving with weapons it is overcome,
but by doing what is holy it overcomes.

In the beginning relying on its own arms the Church gained
Africa, took possession of Europe, occupied Asia. Not by war,
not by the sword, but by the deeds of religion and the reputation
for sanctity the Church carried the Christian banners throughout
the entire world. But when the Bride, who at that time everywhere
was called, brought forth, and greatly desired in her golden robes,
exchanged the golden cloak of the burning spirit for the iron
weapons of a mad Ajax, she lost the power born of the blood of
the twelve Apostles, she abandoned Asia and Jerusalem, she was
forced to relinquish Africa and Egypt, and she saw a good part of
Europe together with the Byzantine Empire and Greece taken
from her. It is the voice of God telling us that when Moses' hands
grow weary and prayers and offerings cease Joshua is conquered
and Amalec triumphs. So we see that when religion exchanges
offerings for the sword in virtually the whole world the Church is
struck, cast forth, and rejected to the immense profit of Mohammed, who, unless the sword is put down and we return again into
the bosom of piety at the altars and the shrines of God, will grow
stronger day by day, will subjugate all to his power, and as the
wicked avenger of our impiety will take possession of the entire
world.

I see, yes, I see that, unless by this Council or by some other
means we place a limit on our morals, unless we force our greedy
desire for human things, the source of evils, to yield to the love of
divine things, it is all over with Christendom, all over with
religion, even all over with those very resources which our fathers
acquired by their greater service of God, but which we are about

to lose because of our neglect. For from extreme poverty these resources became most abundant in such a way that they seem not so long after about to perish, and unless we sound the signal for retreat, unless we have regard for our interests, this most rich fillet,[5] which had served to decorate the heads of the priests, will be found hardly to cover them. Hear the divine voices everywhere sounding, everywhere demanding a Council, peace, that holy enterprise [against the Moslems]. When has our life been more effeminate? When has ambition been more unrestrained, greed more burning? When has the license to sin been more shameless? When has temerity in speaking, in arguing, in writing against piety been more common or more unafraid? When has there been among the people not only a greater neglect but a greater contempt for the sacred, for the sacraments, for the keys [of forgiveness of sins], and for the holy commandments? When have our religion and faith been more open to the derision even of the lowest classes? When, O sorrow, has there been a more disastrous split in the Church? When have war been more dangerous, the enemy more powerful, armies more cruel? When have the signs, portents, and prodigies both of a threatening heaven and of a terrified earth appeared more numerous or more horrible? When (alas, tears hold me back) have the slaughter and destruction been bloodier than at Brescia or at Ravenna? When, I say, did any day among accursed days dawn with more grief or calamity than that most holy day of the Resurrection?[6]

If we are not without feeling, what, pray, are all these things but words sent from heaven? For, as Proclus says, the words of God are deeds, and the prophecies declare "He spoke and they were created" [Ps. 148:5]. In the sacred writings of the Jews, in the ten declarations contained in Genesis,[7] we read that the whole world was created. Therefore, what we are witnessing are words, the words of God warning and instructing you to hold a Council,

---

[5] The term fillet is used by extension (and in a classical sense) to signify the wealth and possessions of the Church.

[6] The battle of Ravenna, a most sanguinary one, took place on the Easter Sunday preceding Egidio's address by just three weeks.

[7] I.e., the ten parts beginning "God said" in Gen. 1.

to reform the Church, to end war between men, to restore peace to your Bride assailed on every side, to avert the sword threatening the throat of the city and of Italy, and to curb our unbridled living which afflicts the heart of the Church with very great wounds.

For it is of no importance how much land we own, but rather how just, how holy, how eager for divine things we are, so that finally after so many evils, so many hardships, and so many calamities, you may hear Christ our Lord making known to Peter and to posterity that the Council is the one and only remedy for all evils, the sole port for the ship in distress, the single means of strengthening the commonweal. He says: "Thou, Peter, being once converted, confirm thy brethren" [Luke 22:32]. Do you hear, Peter? Do you hear, Paul? Do you hear, O most holy heads, protectors and defenders of the city of Rome? Do you hear into what a mass of evils the Church founded in your blood has been led? Do you see the wretched battle line on both sides? Do you see the slaughter? Do you see the destruction? Do you see the battlefield buried under piles of the slain? Do you see that in this year the earth has drunk more gore than water, less rain than blood? Do you see that as much Christian strength lay in the grave as would be enough to wage war against the enemy of the faith and that nothing but ruin and destruction remain for us? Bring us aid, help us, succor us, as you plucked the Church from the jaws of the Jews and the tyrants, raise it up now as it falls under the weight of its own disasters.

The people pray, men, women, every age, both sexes, the entire world. The Fathers ask, the Senate entreats, finally the pope himself as a suppliant implores you to preserve him, the Church, the city of Rome, these temples, these altars, these your own principal shrines, and to make strong the Lateran Council, proclaimed today in your presence by the Supreme Pontiff Julius II (may it be auspicious, happy, and favorable for us, for your Church, and for all of Christendom), that it may accomplish under the power of the Holy Spirit the surest salvation of the world. We beg you to see to it that the Christian princes are brought to peace and the arms of our kings turned against Mohammed, the public enemy of Christ, and not only that the fire of charity of the Church is not extinguished by these waves and storms, but that by the merits of the saving Cross and under the guidance of the Holy Spirit, which are jointly commemorated today, it is cleansed from every stain it has received and is restored to its ancient splendor and purity.

2

Cardinal Ximenes' Dedicatory Prologue to the Complutensian Polyglot Bible 1517

The Complutensian Polyglot was the first Bible to be printed and published in all its original languages—Greek, Hebrew, and Chaldean, as well as the Latin Vulgate—and it is one of the great achievements both of early printing and of humanist scholarship. The project of the Cardinal of Spain, Francisco Ximenes de Cisneros, it was printed at Alcalá (in Latin, Complutum) in six folio volumes in the years 1514 to 1517 but was not actually published until 1522. Ximenes dedicated the work to Pope Leo X, and this dedicatory Prologue or Preface follows the title page in Volume I, the first of the Old Testament volumes. It is a forthright statement of the need to go back to the sources, to the original texts of Holy Scripture. The translation is by John C. Olin.

To Our Most Holy and Most Clement Lord, Leo X,
by Divine Providence Supreme Pontiff,
from the most Reverend Father in Christ and Lord,
by the Grace of God, Francisco Ximenes de Cisneros,
Titular Cardinal Priest of St. Balbina of the Holy Roman
　　Church,
Cardinal of Spain, Archbishop of Toledo,
Archchancellor of the Kingdoms of Castile, etc.

PROLOGUE
to the Books of the Old and New Testaments Printed in
Their Various Languages.

There are many reasons, Holy Father, that impel us to print the
languages of the original text of Holy Scripture. These are the
principal ones. Words have their own unique character, and no
translation of them, however complete, can entirely express their
full meaning. This is especially the case in that language through
which the Lord Himself spoke. The letter here of itself may be
dead and like flesh which profits nought ("for it is the spirit that
gives life" [2 Cor. 3:6]) because Christ concealed by the form of
the words remains enclosed within its womb. But there is no
doubt that there is a rich fecundity so astonishing and an abundance of sacred mysteries so teeming that since it is ever full to
overflowing "streams of living water shall flow out from His
breast" [John 7:38]. And from this source those to whom it has
been given "to behold the glory of the Lord with an unveiled face
and thus be transformed into that very image" [2 Cor. 3:18] can
continually draw the marvelous secrets of His divinity. Indeed
there can be no language or combination of letters from which
the most hidden meanings of heavenly wisdom do not emerge and
burgeon forth, as it were. Since, however, the most learned
translator can present only a part of this, the full Scripture in
translation inevitably remains up to the present time laden with a
variety of sublime truths which cannot be understood from any
source other than the original language.

Moreover, wherever there is diversity in the Latin manuscripts
or the suspicion of a corrupted reading (we know how frequently
this occurs because of the ignorance and negligence of copyists),
it is necessary to go back to the original source of Scripture, as St.
Jerome and St. Augustine and other ecclesiastical writers advise us
to do, to examine the authenticity of the books of the Old
Testament in the light of the correctness of the Hebrew text and
of the New Testament in the light of the Greek copies. And so
that every student of Holy Scripture might have at hand the

original texts themselves and be able to quench his thirst at the very fountainhead of the water that flows unto life everlasting and not have to content himself with rivulets alone, we ordered the original languages of Holy Scripture with their translations adjoined to be printed and dedicated to your Holiness. And we first took care to print the New Testament in Greek and Latin together with a lexicon of all the Greek expressions that can help those reading that language. Thus we spared no effort on behalf of those who have not acquired a full knowledge of the Greek tongue. Then before we began the Old Testament we prepared a dictionary of the Hebrew and Chaldean words of the entire Old Instrument.[1] There not only the various meanings of each expression are given, but (we believe this will be most useful to students) the place in Scripture where each meaning occurs is cited.

Also, since not only the shell of the letter that kills but above all the kernel of the life-giving spirit that lies hidden within must be sought by the student of Holy Scripture, and since an important part of this derives from the translation of proper names, we ordered that their translation be worked out with the greatest care by men who excelled in the knowledge of languages and that they be arranged alphabetically and the list appended to the dictionary. The ascribing of these names, foreseen from eternity, is of incredible help in revealing spiritual and concealed meanings and uncovering hidden mysteries that the Holy Spirit has veiled under the shadow of the literal text. After this list come instruction in reading the Hebrew characters and a grammar of that language compiled from many Hebrew authors of accepted reliability and arranged according to the Latin method.

After we completed all this as a prelude, so to speak, we printed the different languages of the Old Testament and added the Latin translation for each of them. We can frankly state, Most Holy Father, that the greatest part of our labor was expended here. We employed men the most outstanding for their knowledge of languages, and we had the most accurate and the oldest manu-

---

[1]It is interesting to note that Erasmus entitled the first edition of his New Testament in 1516 *Novum Instrumentum*, a term used also by St. Jerome and St. Augustine. The Latin term *instrumentum* is a written document stipulating a pact or covenant. See Bentley, *Humanists and Holy Writ*, p. 121.

scripts for our base texts. We made the greatest effort to gather from various places a large number of Hebrew as well as Greek and Latin codices. Indeed we are indebted to your Holiness for the Greek texts. With the greatest kindness you sent us the most ancient codices of both the Old and the New Testaments from your Apostolic Library, and these were of the greatest help to us in this undertaking.[2]

And so, having completed the printing of the New Testament in Greek and Latin together with its lexicon and also the Hebrew and Chaldean dictionary, to which we appended a grammar as well as the translation of proper names, and in addition having finished annotating variant readings in the Old Testament, annotations which our scholars added in many places since Nicholas of Lyra had not fully completed the task,[3] at last with divine assistance we printed the Old Testament in its various languages. We now send this entire work to your Holiness, for to whom should all our vigilant efforts be dedicated than to that Apostolic See to whom we owe everything? Or who with greater joy ought to accept and embrace the sacred books of the Christian religion than the sacred Vicar of Christ? May your Holiness receive, therefore, with a joyful heart this humble gift which we offer unto the Lord so that the hitherto dormant study of Holy Scripture may now at last begin to revive.

We beseech your Blessedness most earnestly, however, that you examine these books that now prostrate themselves before you and pass the most severe judgment on them so that, if it seems they will be of use to the Christian commonwealth, they may receive permission from your Holiness to be published. We have held them back until now, waiting to consult that sacred oracle of the Apostolic Office. But let this suffice for your Blessedness. We turn now to instruct the reader about the make-up of this work.

---

[2]For reference to the Complutensian manuscripts, see ibid., pp. 92–94.

[3]Nicholas of Lyra (ca. 1270–1340) is the most famous medieval biblical scholar and commentator. His principal work, *Postilla litteralis*, first printed in Rome in 1471–1472, was widely published and very popular.

3

The *Consilium*
de emendanda ecclesia
1537

The *Consilium* is the report of a reform comission which Pope Paul III convened at Rome in late 1536. It met under the presidency of Cardinal Gasparo Contarini, and consisted of some of the most important figures in the story of Catholic reform. The report was formally presented to the pope in March 1537 and is a surprisingly frank and incisive attack on the venality and other abuses associated with the curial system. As Pastor declares, "the wounds had been laid bare, and now the remedy could be applied."[1]

The English text of the *Consilium* has been reprinted from CR, chap. 13, where there is also additional bibliographical information. The original Latin text is in *Concilium Tridentinum*, XII 131–45.

MOST HOLY FATHER, we are so far from being able to express in words the great thanks the Christian Commonwealth should render to Almighty God because He has appointed you pope in these times and pastor of His flock and has given you that resolve which you have that we scarcely hope we can do justice in thought to the gratitude we owe God. For that Spirit of God by whom the power of the heavens has been established, as the prophet says, has

---

[1]Pastor, XI 171.

determined to rebuild through you the Church of Christ, totter-
ing, nay, in fact collapsed, and, as we see, to apply your hand to
this ruin, and to raise it up to its original height and restore it to
its pristine beauty. We shall hope to make the surest interpretation
of this divine purpose—we whom your Holiness has called to
Rome and ordered to make known to you, without regard for
your advantage or for anyone else's, those abuses, indeed those
most serious diseases, which now for a long time afflict God's
Church and especially this Roman Curia and which have now led
with these diseases gradually becoming more troublesome and
destructive to this great ruin which we see.

And your Holiness, taught by the Spirit of God who (as
Augustine says) speaks in hearts without the din of words, had
rightly acknowledged that the origin of these evils was due to the
fact that some popes, your predecessors, in the words of the
Apostle Paul, "having itching ears heaped up to themselves teachers according to their own lusts" [2 Tim. 4:3], not that they might
learn from them what they should do, but that they might find
through the application and cleverness of these teachers a justification for what it pleased them to do. Thence it came about,
besides the fact that flattery follows all dominion as the shadow
does the body and that truth's access to the ears of princes has
always been most difficult, that teachers at once appeared who
taught that the pope is the lord of all benefices and that therefore,
since a lord may sell by right what is his own, it necessarily
follows that the pope cannot be guilty of simony. Thus the will
of the pope, of whatever kind it may be, is the rule governing his
activities and deeds: whence it may be shown without doubt that
whatever is pleasing is also permitted.

From this source as from a Trojan horse so many abuses and
such grave diseases have rushed in upon the Church of God that
we now see her afflicted almost to the despair of salvation and the
news of these things spread even to the infidels (let your Holiness
believe those who know), who for this reason especially deride the
Christian religion, so that through us—through us, we say—the
name of Christ is blasphemed among the heathens.

But you, Most Holy Father, and truly Most Holy, instructed by
the Spirit of God, and with more than that former prudence of
yours, since you have devoted yourself fully to the task of curing

the ills and restoring good health to the Church of Christ committed to your care, you have seen, and you have rightly seen, that the cure must begin where the disease had its origin, and having followed the teaching of the Apostle Paul you wish to be a steward, not a master, and to be found trustworthy by the Lord, having indeed imitated that servant in the Gospel whom the master set over his household to give them their ration of grain in due time [Luke 12:42]; and on that account you have resolved to turn from what is unlawful; nor do you wish to be able to do what you should not. You have therefore summoned us to you, inexperienced indeed and unequal to so great a task, yet not a little disposed both to the honor and glory of your Holiness and especially to the renewal of the Church of Christ; and you have charged us in the gravest language to compile all the abuses and to make them known to you, having solemnly declared that we shall give you an account of this task entrusted to us to Almighty God if we carelessly or unfaithfully execute it. And you have bound us by oath so that we can discuss all these matters more freely and explain them to you, the penalty of excommunication even having been added lest we disclose anything of our office to anyone.

We have therefore made, in obedience to your command and insofar as it can be briefly done, a compilation of those diseases and their remedies—remedies, we stress, which we were able to devise given the limitations of our talents. But you indeed according to your goodness and wisdom will restore and bring to completion all matters where we have been remiss in view of our limitations. And in order to set ourselves some fixed boundaries, since your Holiness is both the prince of those provinces which are under ecclesiastical authority and the pope of the universal Church as well as bishop of Rome, we have not ventured to say anything about matters which pertain to this principality of the Church, excellently ruled, we see, by your prudence. We shall touch, however, on those matters which pertain to the office of universal pontiff and to some extent on those which have to do with the bishop of Rome.

This point, we believed, most Holy Father, must be established before everything else, as Aristotle says in the *Politics*, that in this ecclesiastical government of the Church of Christ just as in every body politic this rule must be held supreme, that as far as possible the laws be observed; nor do we think that it is licit for us to dispense from these laws save for a pressing and necessary reason. For no more dangerous custom can be introduced in any commonwealth than this failure to observe the laws, which our ancestors wished to be sacred and whose authority they called venerable and divine. You know all this, excellent Pontiff; you have long ago read this in the philosophers and theologians. Indeed we think that the following precept is not only most germane to this, but a greater and higher ordinance by far, that it cannot be permitted even for the Vicar of Christ to obtain any profit in the use of the power of the keys conferred on him by Christ. For truly this is the command of Christ: "Freely you have received, freely give" [Matt. 10:8].

These points having been established at the outset, then [it should be remembered] your Holiness takes care of the Church of Christ with the help of a great many servants through whom he exercises this responsibility. These, moreover, are all clerics to whom divine worship has been entrusted, priests especially and particularly parish priests and above all bishops. Therefore, if this government is to proceed properly, care must be taken that these servants are qualified for the office which they must discharge.

The first abuse in this respect is the ordination of clerics and especially of priests in which no care is taken, no diligence employed, so that indiscriminately the most unskilled, men of the vilest stock and of evil morals, adolescents, are admitted to Holy Orders and to the priesthood, to the [indelible] mark, we stress, which above all denotes Christ. From this have come innumerable scandals and a contempt for the ecclesiastical order, and reverence for divine worship not only has been diminished but has almost by now been destroyed. Therefore, we think that it would be an excellent thing if your Holiness first in this city of Rome appointed two or three prelates, learned and upright men, to preside over the ordination of clerics. Your Holiness should also instruct all bishops, even under pain of censure, to give careful attention to this in their own dioceses. Nor should your Holiness allow anyone to be ordained except by his own bishop or with the permission of deputies in Rome or of his own bishop. Moreover, we think that each bishop should have a teacher in his diocese to instruct clerics in minor orders both in letters and in morals, as the laws prescribe.

Another abuse of the greatest consequence is in the bestowing of ecclesiastical benefices, especially parishes and above all bishoprics, in the matter of which the practice has become entrenched that provision is made for the persons on whom the benefices are bestowed, but not for the flock and Church of Christ. Therefore, in bestowing parish benefices, but above all bishoprics, care must be taken that they be given to good and learned men so that they themselves can perform those duties to which they are bound, and, in addition, that they be conferred on those who will in all likelihood reside.[2] A benefice in Spain or in Britain then must not be conferred on an Italian, or vice versa. This must be observed both in appointments to benefices vacated through death and in the case of resignations, where now only the intention of the person resigning is considered and nothing else. In the case of these resignations we think that it would have good effect if one or several upright men were put in charge of the matter.

Another abuse, when benefices are bestowed or turned over to others, has crept in in connection with the arrangement of payments from the income of these benefices. Indeed, the person resigning the benefice often reserves all the income for himself.[3] In such cases care must be taken that payments can be reserved for no other reason and with no other justification than for alms which ought to be given for pious uses and for the needy. For income is joined to the benefice as the body to the soul. By its very nature then it belongs to him who holds the benefice so that he can live from it respectably according to his station and can at the same time support the expenses for divine worship and for the upkeep of the church and other religious buildings, and so that he may expend what remains for pious uses. For this is the nature of the income of these benefices. But just as in the course of natural

---

[2]Regarding this important question see Adrian VI's concluding remarks in his Instruction to Chieregati, in CR, chap. 9.

[3]Luther's gloss on this particular passage, which is characteristic of his remarks in general on the *Consilium*, reads as follows: "This Romish trick was invented by the popes and cardinals themselves, and it is doubtful that they will be reformed therein." See *Luther's Works*, edd. Helmuth Lehmann, Jaroslav Pelikan, et al., 56 vols. (St. Louis: Concordia, 1955—), xxxiv 248.

events some things occur in particular cases which are contrary to the tendency of nature as a whole, so in the instance of the pope, because he is the universal steward of the goods of the Church, if he sees that that portion of the revenues which should be spent for pious uses or a part of it may more usefully be spent for some other pious purpose, he can without a doubt arrange it. He is able, therefore, in all justice to set aside payment to aid a person in need, especially a cleric, so that he can live respectably according to his station. For that reason it is a great abuse when all revenues are reserved and everything is taken away which should be allotted to divine service and to the support of him who holds the benefice. And likewise it is certainly a great abuse to make payments to rich clerics who can live satisfactorily and respectably on the income they have. Both abuses must be abolished.

Still another abuse is in the exchanging of benefices which occur under agreements that are all simoniacal and with no consideration except for the profit.

Another abuse must be entirely removed which has now become prevalent in this Curia due to a certain cunning on the part of some experienced persons. For, although the law provides that benefices cannot be bequeathed in a will, since they belong not to the testator but to the Church, and this so that these ecclesiastical properties may be kept in common for the benefit of all and not become the private possession of anyone, human diligence—but not Christian diligence—has discovered a great many ways whereby this law may be mocked. For first the surrender of bishoprics and other benefices are made with the right of regaining them [cum regressu]; the reservation of the income is added, then the reservation of conferring benefices; the reservation of the administration is piled on top of this, and by this stipulation they make him bishop who does not have the rights of a bishop, whereas all the episcopal rights are given to him who is not made bishop. May your Holiness see how far this flattering teaching has advanced, where at length it has led, so that what is pleasing is permitted. What, I pray, is this except appointing an heir for oneself to a benefice? Besides this another trick has been devised, when coadjutors are given to bishops requesting them, men less qualified than they themselves are, so that, unless one wishes to close his eyes, he may clearly see that by this means an heir is appointed.

Also, an ancient law was renewed by Clement [VII] that sons of priests may not have the benefices of their fathers, lest in this way the common property [of the Church] become private property. Nevertheless, dispensations are made (so we hear) in the case of this law which ought to be revered. We have not been willing to be silent in the face of that which any prudent man may judge for himself to be absolutely true, namely, that nothing has stirred up more this ill-will toward the clergy, whence so many quarrels have arisen and others threaten, than this diversion of ecclesiastical revenues and income from the general to private advantage. Formerly everyone was hopeful [that such abuses would be corrected]; now led to despair they sharpen their tongues against this See.

Another abuse is in the matter of expectatives and reservations of benefices,[4] and the occasion is given to desire another's death and to hear of it with pleasure. Indeed the more worthy are excluded when there are vacancies, and cause is given for litigations. All these abuses, we think, must be abolished.

Another abuse has been devised with the same cunning. For certain benefices are by right "incompatible," and they are so designated. By virtue of that term our forefathers have wished to remind us that they should not be conferred on one single person. Now dispensations are granted in these cases not only for two [such benefices] but for more, and, what is worse, for bishoprics. We feel that this custom which has become so prevalent because of greed must be abolished, especially in the case of bishoprics. What about the lifelong unions of benefices in one man, so that such a plurality of benefices is no obstacle to holding benefices that are "incompatible"? Is that not a pure betrayal of the law?

Another abuse has also become prevalent, that bishoprics are conferred on the most reverend cardinals or that not one but several are put in their charge, an abuse, most Holy Father, which we think is of great importance in God's Church. In the first place, because the offices of cardinal and bishop are "incompatible." For the cardinals are to assist your Holiness in governing the

---

[4] An expectative is the assignment of a benefice before it has become vacant. A reservation of a benefice is the retention of the right to assign it.

universal Church; the bishop's duty, however, is to tend his own flock, which he cannot do well and as he should unless he lives with his sheep as a shepherd with his flock.

Furthermore, Holy Father, this practice is especially injurious in the example it sets. For how can this Holy See set straight and correct the abuses of others if abuses are tolerated in its own principal members? Nor do we think that because they are cardinals they have a greater license to transgress the law; on the contrary, they have far less. For the life of these men ought to be a law for others; nor should they imitate the Pharisees who speak and do not act, but Christ our Savior who began to act and afterward to teach. This practice is more harmful in the deliberations of the Church, for this license nurtures greed. Besides, the cardinals solicit bishoprics from kings and princes, on whom they are afterward dependent and about whom they cannot freely pass judgment. Indeed, even if they are able and willing, they are nevertheless led astray, confused in their judgment by their partisanship. Would that this custom be abolished therefore and provision be made that the cardinals can live respectably in accordance with their dignity, each receiving an equal income. We believe that this can easily be done if we wish to abandon the servitude to Mammon and to serve only Christ.

With these abuses corrected which pertain to the appointment of your ministers, through whom as through instruments both the worship of God can be properly directed and the Christian people well instructed and governed in the Christian life, we must now approach those matters which refer to the government of the Christian people. In this regard, most blessed Father, the abuse that first and before all others must be reformed is that bishops above all and then parish priests must not be absent from their churches and parishes except for some grave reason, but must reside, especially bishops, as we have said, because they are the bridegrooms of the church entrusted to their care. For, by the Eternal God, what sight can be more lamentable for the Christian man traveling through the Christian world than this desertion of the churches? Nearly all the shepherds have departed from their flocks; nearly all have been entrusted to hirelings.[5] A heavy pen-

---

[5]"The calamity of our age," says Contarini, with reference to such widespread absenteeism and neglect, in his *De officio episcopi*; see CR, chap. 7.

alty, therefore, must be imposed on bishops before the others, and then on parish priests, who are absent from their flocks, not only censures, but also the withholding of the income of absentees, unless the bishops have obtained permission from your Holiness and the parish priests from their bishops to be away for a short period of time. Some laws and the decrees of some Councils may be read in this regard, which provide that the bishop shall not be permitted to be away from his church for more than three Sundays.

It is also an abuse that so many of the most reverend cardinals are absent from this Curia and perform none of the duties incumbent on them as cardinals. Although perhaps not all should reside here, for we think it advantageous that some should live in their provinces—for through them as through some roots spread out into the whole Christian world the peoples are bound together under this Roman See—yet your Holiness therefore should call most to the Curia that they might reside here. For in this way, aside from the fact that the cardinals would be performing their office, provision would also be made for the dignity of the Curia and the gap repaired, if any should occur by the withdrawal of many bishops returning to their own churches.

Another great abuse and one that must by no means be tolerated, whereby the whole Christian people is scandalized, arises from the obstacles the bishops face in the government of their flocks, especially in punishing and correcting evildoers. For in the first place wicked men, chiefly clerics, free themselves in many ways from the jurisdiction of their ordinary. Then, if they have not arranged this exemption, they at once have recourse to the Penitentiary or to the Datary, where they immediately find a way to escape punishment, and, what is worse, they find this in consideration of the payment of money. This scandal, most blessed Father, so greatly disturbs the Christian people that words cannot express it. Let these abuses be abolished, we implore your Holiness by the Blood of Christ, by which He has redeemed for Himself His Church and in which He has bathed her. Let these stains be removed, by which, if any access were given to them in any commonwealth of men or any kingdom, it would at once or very soon fall headlong into ruin; nor could it in any way longer survive. Yet we think that we are at liberty to introduce these monstrosities into the Christian Commonwealth.

. Another abuse must be corrected with regard to the religious orders, for many have become so deformed that they are a great scandal to the laity and do grave harm by their example. We think that all conventual orders ought to be done away with, not however that injury be done to anyone, but by prohibiting the admission of novices. Thus they might be quickly abolished without wronging anyone, and good religious could be substituted for them. In fact, we now think that it would be best if all boys who have not been professed were removed from their monasteries.[6]

We believe that the appointment of preachers and confessors from among the friars must also be given attention and corrected, first that their superiors take great care that they are qualified and then that they are presented to the bishops, to whom above all others the care of the Church has been entrusted, by whom they may be examined either directly or through capable men. Nor should they be permitted to carry out these tasks without the consent of the bishops.

We have said, most blessed Father, that it is not lawful in any way in the matter of the use of the keys for him exercising this power to obtain any profit. Concerning this there is the firm word of Christ: "Freely you have received, freely give." This pertains not only to your Holiness, but to all who share your power. Therefore we would wish that this same injunction be observed by the legates and nuncios. For just as custom which has now become prevalent dishonors this See and disturbs the people, so, if the contrary were done, this See would win the highest honor and the people would be wonderfully edified.

Another abuse troubles the Christian people with regard to nuns under the care of conventual friars, where in very many

---

[6]The *Consilium* quite clearly is not recommending "the abolition of monasticism," as H. R. Trevor-Roper states it is in his *Historical Essays* (New York: Harper & Row, 1966), p. 50. It is simply a matter of doing away with the relaxed or less strict branches of the mendicant orders, notably the Franciscan Conventuals. In fact, the reform of monasticism and the establishment of new orders— the Theatines, the Capuchins, and later the Jesuits—had major support among the authors of the *Consilium*.

convents public sacrilege occurs with the greatest scandal to all. Therefore, let your Holiness take this entire responsibility away from the conventuals and give it either to the ordinaries or to others, whatever will be deemed better.

There is a great and dangerous abuse in the public schools, especially in Italy, where many professors of philosophy teach ungodly things. Indeed, the most ungodly disputations take place in the churches, and, if they are of a religious nature, what pertains to the divine in them is treated before the people with great irreverence. We believe, therefore, that the bishops must be instructed, where there are public schools, to admonish those who lecture that they not teach the young ungodly things, but that they show the weakness of the natural light [of reason] in questions relating to God, to the newness or the eternity of the world, and the like, and guide these youths to what is godly. Likewise, that public disputations on questions of this kind should not be permitted, nor on theological matters either, which disputations certainly destroy much respect among the common people, but that disputations on these matters be held privately and on other questions in the realm of natural science publicly. And the same charge must be imposed on all other bishops, especially of important cities, where disputations of this kind are wont to be held.

The same care must also be employed in the printing of books, and all princes should be instructed by letter to be on their guard lest any books be printed indiscriminately under their authority. Responsibility in this matter should be given to the ordinaries. And because boys in elementary school are now accustomed to read the *Colloquies* of Erasmus, in which there is much to educate unformed minds to ungodly things, the reading of this book and others of this type then must be prohibited in grammar school.[7]

---

[7]Erasmus' *Colloquies* was first published in 1518 and saw numerous editions and enlargements in subsequent years. Originally intended as a school text, it became one of Erasmus' most popular works. Because of its ridicule and criticism of many common practices and notably of the monks and friars, it came under frequent attack. Its censure by the Sorbonne in 1526 elicited a defense of it by Erasmus, which may be read in *The Colloquies of Erasmus*, trans. Craig R. Thompson (Chicago: The University of Chicago Press, 1965), Appendix I. In view of other condemnations, the above prohibition, limited as it is to grammar schools, is rather mild.

Following these matters which pertain to the instruction of your ministers in the care of the universal Church and in its administration, it must be noted that with regard to privileges granted by your Holiness besides the former abuses other abuses have also been introduced.

The first concerns renegade friars or religious who after a solemn vow withdraw from their order and obtain permission not to wear the habit of their order or even the trace of a habit, but only dignified clerical dress. Let us omit for the moment any reference to gain. For we have already said in the beginning that it is not lawful to make a profit for oneself from the use of the keys and of the power given by Christ, but that one must abstain from this indulgence. For the habit is the sign of profession, whence a dispensation cannot be given even by the bishop to whom these renegades are subject. Therefore this privilege ought not to be granted them; nor should those, when they depart from a vow which binds them to God, be allowed to hold benefices or administrative posts.

Another abuse concerns the pardoners [of the hospital] of the Holy Spirit, [of the hospital] of St. Anthony, and others of this type, who deceive the peasants and simple people and ensnare them with innumerable superstitions.[8] It is our opinion that these pardoners should be abolished.

Another abuse is in connection with dispensing a person established in Holy Orders so that he can take a wife. This dispensation should not be given anyone except for the preservation of a people or a nation, where there is a most serious public reason, especially in these times when the Lutherans lay such great stress on this matter.

There is an abuse in dispensing in the case of marriages between those related by blood or by marriage. Indeed we do not think that this should be done within the second degree [of consanguinity] except for a serious public reason and in other degrees except for a good reason and without any payment of money, as we have already said, unless the parties previously have been united in

---

[8]The pardoners mentioned were attached to two hospitals in Rome. There were many complaints about the kind of indulgence-preaching these and similar pardoners conducted. See *Concilium Tridentinum*, XII 142n1.

marriage. In that case it may be permitted in view of the absolution of a sin already committed to impose a money fine after absolution and to allot it to the pious causes to which your Holiness contributes. For just as no money can be demanded when the use of the keys is without sin, so a money fine can be imposed and allotted to pious usage when absolution from sin is sought.

Another abuse concerns the absolution of those guilty of simony. Alas, how this destructive vice holds sway in the Church of God, so that some have no fear of committing simony and then immediately seek absolution from punishment. Indeed they purchase that absolution, and thus they retain the benefice which they have purchased. We do not say that your Holiness is not able to absolve them of that punishment which has been ordained by positive law, but that he ought by no means to do so, so that opposition might be offered to a crime so great that there is none more dangerous or more scandalous.

Also permission should not be given to clerics to bequeath ecclesiastical property except for an urgent reason, lest the possessions of the poor be converted to private pleasure and the enlarging of a person's own estate.

Moreover confessional letters as well as the use of portable altars should not be readily allowed, for this cheapens the devotions of the Church and the most important sacrament of all. Nor should indulgences be granted except once a year in each of the principal cities. And the commutation of vows ought not to be so easily made, except in view of an equivalent good.

It has also been the custom to alter the last wills of testators who bequeath a sum of money for pious causes, which amount is transferred by the authority of your Holiness to an heir or legatee because of alleged poverty, etc., but actually because of greed. Indeed, unless there has been a great change in the household affairs of an heir because of the death of the testator, so that it is likely that the testator would have altered his will in view of that situation, it is wicked to alter the wills of testators. We have already spoken often about greed, wherefore we think that this practice should be entirely avoided.

Having set forth in brief all those matters which pertain to the pontiff of the universal Church as far as we could comprehend them, we shall in conclusion say something about that which pertains to the bishop of Rome. This city and church of Rome is the mother and teacher of the other churches. Therefore in her especially divine worship and integrity of morals ought to flourish. Accordingly, most blessed Father, all strangers are scandalized when they enter the basilica of St. Peter where priests, some of whom are vile, ignorant, and clothed in robes and vestments which they cannot decently wear in poor churches, celebrate mass. This is a great scandal to everyone. Therefore the most reverend archpriest or the most reverend penitentiary must be ordered to attend to this matter and remove this scandal. And the same must be done in other churches.

Also in this city harlots walk about like matrons or ride on mules, attended in broad daylight by noble members of the cardinals' households and by clerics. In no city do we see this corruption except in this model for all cities. Indeed they even dwell in fine houses. This foul abuse must also be corrected.

There are also in this city the hatreds and animosities of private citizens which it is especially the concern of the bishop to compose and conciliate. Therefore, all these animosities must be resolved and the passions of the citizens composed by some cardinals, Romans especially, who are more qualified.

There are in this city hospitals, orphans, widows. Their care especially is the concern of the bishop and the prince. Therefore your Holiness could properly take care of all of these through cardinals who are upright men.

These are the abuses, most blessed Father, which for the present, according to the limitations of our talents, we thought should be compiled, and which seemed to us ought to be corrected. You indeed, in accord with your goodness and wisdom, will direct all these matters. We certainly, if we have not done justice to the magnitude of the task which is far beyond our powers, have nevertheless satisfied our consciences, and we are not without the greatest hope that under your leadership we may see the Church of God cleansed, beautiful as a dove, at peace with herself, agreeing in one body, to the eternal memory of your name. You have taken the name of Paul; you will imitate, we hope, the charity of Paul. He was chosen as the vessel to carry the name of Christ among the nations [Acts 9:15]. Indeed, we hope that you have been chosen to restore in our hearts and in our works the name of

Christ now forgotten by the nations and by us clerics, to heal the
ills, to lead back the sheep of Christ into one fold, to turn away
from us the wrath of God and that vengeance which we deserve,
already prepared and looming over our heads.

    Gasparo, Cardinal Contarini
    Gian Pietro [Carafa], Cardinal of Chieti
    Jacopo, Cardinal Sadoleto
    Reginald [Pole], Cardinal of England
    Federigo [Fregoso], Archbishop of Salerno
    Jerome [Aleander], Archbishop of Brindisi
    Gian Matteo [Giberti], Bishop of Verona
    Gregorio [Cortese], Abbot of San Giorgio, Venice
    Friar Tommaso [Badia], Master of the Sacred Palace[9]

---

[9]The question of who actually wrote the *Consilium* has often been discussed,
and various attributions have been made (see ibid., 132–33). Given the state of
the problem, however, it seems best to attribute it to the nine signatories as a
collective work, though perhaps Contarini and Carafa may be viewed as the
principal authors. A strong case can be made especially for the latter, in view of
his energetic personality and of several important points of similarity between
the *Consilium* and a reform memorial he sent to Clement VII in 1532. This latter
document may be found in ibid., 67–77, and is discussed in G. M. Monti,
Ricerche su Papa Paolo IV Carafa I (Benevento: Cooperativi Typographi, 1923),
where (pp. 41–47) its correspondence with the *Consilium* is stressed.

4

Jesuit Beginnings

A Letter to Diego de Gouvea from Pierre Favre and Companions
1538

Diego de Gouvea was the principal of the College of Sainte-Barbe
in Paris which Ignatius Loyola, Pierre Favre, Francis Xavier, and
Simon Rodrigues had attended. He was Portuguese and was frequently engaged in diplomatic tasks for the Portuguese king, John
III. Early in 1538 he wrote to the king to suggest that he obtain the
services of Ignatius and his friends to help evangelize the Indies,
and he later wrote to the companions themselves in Rome, urging
them to go to the Indies. The letter published here is their reply.
They stress that they have now put themselves at the disposal of
the pope. Gouvea sent this letter to the king, who in August 1539
instructed his ambassador in Rome to inquire about the possible
enlistment of these men for missionary work. The upshot of the
negotiations that followed was the sending of Francis Xavier to
India and the beginnings of the vast Jesuit missionary enterprise.

   The letter has been reprinted from *The Autobiography of St.
Ignatius Loyola*, ed. Olin, Appendix II. It was translated from the
Latin text in *Monumenta Historica Societatis Iesu. Monumenta Ignatiana*. I. *Sancti Ignatii de Loyola, Societatis Iesu fundatoris, epistolae et
instructiones*, 11 vols. (Madrid: López, 1903–1911), I 132–34.

IHS

May the grace of our Lord Jesus Christ and peace be with all.

A few days ago your messenger arrived here with your letter to us. From him we heard the news concerning you, and from the letter we learned of your excellent recollection of us as well as of the great desire you have for the salvation of those souls in your Indies which are becoming white for the harvest. Would that we could satisfy you and moreover our own inclinations which are likewise zealous! But something at present stands in the way so that we cannot respond to the desires of many, to say nothing of yours. You will understand this from what I now explain. All of us who are mutually bound together in this Society have pledged ourselves to the supreme pontiff, seeing that he is the lord of the entire harvest of Christ. In this offering we have indicated to him that we are prepared for all that he may in Christ decide in our case. If, therefore, he should send us there where you summon us, we shall go rejoicing. The reason that we subjected ourselves in this way to his judgment and will was that we know that he has a greater knowledge of what is advantageous to the whole of Christendom.

There have not been lacking some who for a long time now have been trying to have us sent to those Indies which the Spaniards are daily acquiring for the emperor. A certain Spanish bishop and the envoy of the emperor had been especially persistent in this regard, but they learned that it is not the will of the supreme pontiff that we depart from here because even at Rome there is an abundant harvest. To be sure, the distance of places does not frighten us nor does the labor of learning the language. Let only that be done which above all is pleasing to Christ. Ask in our behalf, therefore, that He make us His ministers in the word of life. "There is no question of our being qualified in ourselves" [2 Cor. 3:5]; rather our hope is in His abundance and riches.

You will learn much about us and our affairs from the letter which we have written to our special friend and brother in Christ, Diego de Cáceres, a Spaniard.[1] He will show it to you. There you will see how many tribulations we have hitherto endured at Rome, and how we at last emerged unscathed. Even in Rome there are

---

[1] Cáceres was an early companion who later left the Society. He was at this time completing his studies in Paris.

many to whom the light of the Church's truth and life is hateful. Be you vigilant therefore, and with as much effort occupy yourself now in teaching the Christian people by the example of living as heretofore you exerted in defense of the faith and the Church's teaching. For how do we believe the good God will preserve the truth of the holy faith in us if we flee from virtue itself? It must be feared that the principal cause of errors of doctrine comes from errors of life, which unless they be corrected, the doctrinal errors will not be cleared from the way.

As we bring this letter to an end, it remains for us to beg you to deign to commend us to our most esteemed masters, Barthélemey, de Cornet, Piccard, Adam, Wancob, Laurency, Benoît, and all others, who gladly acknowledge being our teachers and us as their students and sons in Christ Jesus in whom farewell.

From the city of Rome, November 23, 1538

Yours in the Lord,
Pierre Favre and his companions and brothers

The First Sketch of the
Society of Jesus
1539

This sketch or *prima summa* is the earliest statement describing the
new religious order. It was drawn up by Ignatius and his companions after long discussions concerning their purpose and more
formal organization in the spring and summer of 1539. It was
submitted to Pope Paul III, who gave his approval in September. It
was incorporated in the official bull of institution for the Society,
Regimini militantis ecclesiae, which was issued in September 1540.

The statement has been reprinted from *The Autobiography of St.
Ignatius Loyola*, ed. Olin, Appendix III. It was translated from the
Latin text in *Monumenta Historica Societatis Iesu. Monumenta Igna-
tiana. III. Sancti Ignatii de Loyola Constitutiones Societatis Iesu*, 2 vols.
(Rome: Borgo Sancto Spirito V, 1934–1936), I 16–20.

1. Whoever wishes to be a soldier of God under the standard of
the cross and to serve the Lord alone and His Vicar on earth in
our Society, which we desire to be designated by the name of
Jesus, should, after a solemn vow of perpetual chastity, bear in
mind that he is part of a community founded principally for the
advancement of souls in Christian life and doctrine and for the
propagation of the faith by the ministry of the word, by spiritual
exercises, by works of charity, and expressly by the instruction in
Christianity of children and the uneducated. He should especially
direct himself and take care to have always before his eyes first
God, then the plan of this his Institute, which is, as it were, a way
to Him, and to strive with all his strength to attain this goal which
God has set before him, each one, however, according to the grace

given him by the Holy Spirit and the particular grade of his vocation, lest anyone by chance yield to zeal but not with knowledge. The decision about the particular grade of each one and the entire selection and distribution of duties shall be in the hands of the *prepositus* or prelate chosen by us so that the appropriate order necessary in every well-organized community may be preserved. This *prepositus* with the advice of the brothers shall have the authority to establish in council constitutions profitable for the achievement of this goal set before us, a majority of the votes always having the right to decide. In matters that are more serious and lasting, a council should be understood to be the greater part of the whole Society which can conveniently be summoned by the *prepositus*; in lighter and more temporary matters it will be all those who happen to be present in the place where our *prepositus* resides. All right to execute and command, however, will be in the power of the *prepositus*.

2. All the companions should know and daily bear in mind, not only when they first make their profession but as long as they live, that this entire Society and each one individually are soldiers of God under faithful obedience to our most holy lord Paul III and his successors and are thus under the command of the Vicar of Christ and his divine power not only as having the obligation to him which is common to all clerics, but also as being so bound by the bond of a vow that whatever His Holiness commands pertaining to the advancement of souls and the propagation of the faith we must immediately carry out, without any evasion or excuse, as far as in us lies, whether he sends us to the Turks or to the New World or to the Lutherans or to others, be they infidel or faithful. For this reason those who would join us, and before they put their shoulders to this burden, should meditate long and hard whether they possess the spiritual riches to enable them to complete this tower in keeping with the counsel of the Lord, that is, whether the Holy Spirit who incites them promises them sufficient grace so that with His help they may hope to bear the weight of this vocation. And after, with the Lord inspiring them, they have enlisted in this militia of Jesus Christ, they must have their loins girded day and night and be ready to discharge so great a debt. Lest, however, there could be among us any ambition for or rejection of particular missions or assignments, let each one prom-

ise never to take the matter of such missions up with the pontiff either directly or indirectly, but to leave all this care to God and to His Vicar and to the *prepositus* of the Society. The *prepositus*, like the others, shall also promise to take nothing up with the pontiff either one way or another concerning a mission of his own, except with the advice of the Society.

3. Each one shall vow that he will be obedient to the *prepositus* of the Society in all things relevant to the observance of this our rule. The latter, moreover, shall ordain what he deems to be appropriate for achieving the goal set before him by God and the Society. In his office, however, let him always remember the kindness, gentleness, and charity of Christ and the pattern of Peter and Paul, and let both him and the council constantly keep this norm in view. Particularly let them hold esteemed the instruction of children and the uneducated in the Christian doctrine of the Ten Commandments and other similar rudiments, whatever will seem suitable to them in accordance with the circumstances of persons, places, and times. For it is very necessary that the *prepositus* and the council give this matter the most diligent attention since among our neighbors the edifice of faith cannot arise without a foundation and since among us there is the danger that, as anyone becomes more learned, he may attempt to decline this assignment as being at first glance less splendid, although in reality there is none more faithful either for the edification of neighbors or for the practice of the duties of charity and humility in our own case. The subjects, that is, the members of the Society, both for the great utility of the order and for the sake of the continual practice of humility, which has never been sufficiently praised, shall be always bound to obey the *prepositus* in all things pertaining to the Institute of the Society, and they shall acknowledge and venerate as far as it is fitting Christ as though present in him.

4. Since we have learned from experience that a life as far removed as possible from every taint of avarice and as close as possible to evangelical poverty is more joyful, more pure, and more appropriate for the edification of neighbor, and since we know that our Lord Jesus Christ will provide what is necessary for food and clothing for His servants seeking only the Kingdom of God, each and all shall vow perpetual poverty, declaring that they cannot either individually or in common acquire any civil right to any

real property or any revenue or income for the maintenance and use of the Society. Rather let them be content to delight in the use only of the necessary things, with the owners permitting, and to receive money and the value of things given them in order to provide the necessities for themselves. They shall be able, however, to acquire the civil right to real property and to income in order to bring together some talented students and instruct them especially in sacred letters at the universities, that is, for the support of those students who desire to advance in the spirit and in letters and at length to be received in our Society after probation when the period of their studies has been finished.

5. All the companions who are in holy orders, even though they can acquire no right to benefices and incomes, shall be bound to say the office according to the rites of the Church, but not in choir lest they be led away from the works of charity to which we have all dedicated ourselves. For this reason neither organs nor singing shall be used in their masses and religious ceremonies, for these, which laudably adorn the divine worship of the other clerics and religious and have been found to arouse and move souls by virtue of their hymns and rites, we have found to be a considerable hindrance to us, since as a consequence of the nature of our vocation, besides other necessary duties, we must frequently be occupied a great part of the day and even of the night in comforting the sick both in body and in spirit.

These are the features concerning our profession which we are able to explain in a kind of sketch, and we do this now in order to instruct in a brief account both those who question us about our plan of life and also our posterity, if, God willing, we shall ever have imitators of this way. And since we have learned that this way has many and great difficulties connected with it, we have thought it useful to admonish those not to infringe, under the pretext of what is right, upon these two prohibitions. One is that they do not impose on the companions under pain of mortal sin any fasts, disciplines, baring of feet or head, style of dress, type of food, penances, hair shirts, and other torments of the flesh. These, however, we do not therefore prohibit because we condemn them, for we greatly praise and honor them in the men who observe them, but only because we do not wish ours to be crushed by so many burdens at the same time joined together or to allege any excuse for not carrying out what we have set before ourselves.

Everyone can, however, exercise himself faithfully in those practices he deems to be necessary and useful for himself, as long as
the *prepositus* does not prohibit them. The other is that no one be
received into the Society unless he first has been tested for a long
time and most diligently. And when he appears prudent in Christ
and distinguished [*conspicuus*] both in learning and in holiness of
life, then at length let him be admitted to the militia of Jesus
Christ, who may deign to favor our feeble undertakings for the
glory of God the Father, to whom alone be glory and honor
forever. Amen.

5

Reform Decrees of Trent
1563

The two decrees that follow are from the Council of Trent's final period and comprise the substance of its reform legislation. The first was approved at the Twenty-Third Session on July 15, 1563; the second, at the Twenty-Fourth Session on November 11, 1563. I have discussed their content and importance in the essay in the first part of this volume, but attention in particular is called here to the strong statement on residence in Chapter I in the first decree—it embodies the compromise that broke the deadlock on the question at the Council—and to the injunction to establish seminaries for the education of priests in Chapter XVIII of the first decree.

The decrees are reprinted from the English text in Schroeder, pp. 164–79 and 190–212, respectively.

Decree of the Twenty-Third Session

CHAPTER I

THE NEGLIGENCE OF PASTORS OF CHURCHES IN THE MATTER OF RESIDENCE IS IN VARIOUS WAYS RESTRAINED; THE *CURA ANIMARUM* IS PROVIDED FOR

Since by divine precept it is enjoined on all to whom is entrusted the *cura animarum* to know their sheep [John 10:1–16, 21:15–17; Acts 20:28], to offer sacrifice for them, and to feed them by the preaching of the divine word, the administration of the sacraments, and the example of all good works, to exercise a fatherly care in behalf of the poor and other distressed persons, and to apply themselves to all other pastoral duties, all of which cannot be rendered and fulfilled by those who do not watch over and are not with their flock, but desert it after the manner of hirelings [John 10:12f.], the holy Council admonishes and exhorts them that, mindful of the divine precepts and *made a pattern of the flock* [see 1 Peter 5:3], they in judgment and in truth be shepherds and leaders. And lest those things that concern residence which have already been piously and with profit decreed under Paul III, of happy memory, be understood in a sense foreign to the mind of the holy Council, as if in virtue of that decree it were lawful to be absent during five continuous months, the holy Council, adhering to that decree, declares that all who, under whatever name or title, even though they be cardinals of the holy Roman Church, preside over patriarchal, primatial, metropolitan, and cathedral churches, are bound to personal residence in their church or diocese, where they are obligated to discharge the office committed to them and from which they may not absent themselves except for the reasons and in the manner subjoined. Since Christian charity, urgent necessity, due obedience, and manifest advantage to the Church or the commonwealth require and demand that some at times be absent, the same holy Council decrees that these reasons for lawful absence must be approved in writing by the most blessed Roman pontiff, or by the metropolitan, or, in his absence, by the oldest resident suffragan bishop, whose duty it shall also be to approve the absence of the metropolitan; except when the absence is necessitated by some function or office of the state attached to the episcopal dignity, in which cases the absence being a matter of public knowledge and at times unexpected, it will not be necessary to make known to the metropolitan the reasons therefor. To him, however, in conjunction with the provincial council, it shall pertain to decide concerning the permissions granted by himself or by his suffragans and to see that no one abuses that right and that transgressors are punished in accordance with canonical prescriptions. Moreover, those who are about to depart should remember so to provide for their sheep that as far as possible they may not suffer any injury through their absence. But since those who are absent only for a brief period appear in the sense of the ancient canons not to be absent, because they are soon to return, the holy Council wishes that that period of absence in a single year, whether continuous or interrupted, ought, except for the reasons mentioned above, in no case to exceed two or at most three months, and that consideration be taken that it be made from a just cause and without any detriment to the flock. Whether this be the case, the Council leaves to the conscience of those who depart, which it hopes will be religious and delicate, for hearts are open to God [Ps. 7:10; Acts 1:24], whose work they are bound at their peril not to do deceitfully [Jer. 48:10]. Meanwhile it admonishes and exhorts them in the Lord that, unless their episcopal duties call them elsewhere in their diocese, they are on no account to absent themselves from their cathedral church during the periods of the Advent of the Lord, Quadragesima, the Nativity, Easter, Pentecost, and Corpus Christi, on which days especially the sheep ought to be refreshed and to rejoice in the Lord at the presence of the shepherd.

But if anyone, which it is hoped will never happen, shall have been absent in violation of the provision of this decree, the holy Council ordains that in addition to the other penalties imposed upon and renewed against non-residents under Paul III, and the guilt of mortal sin which he incurs, he can acquire no proprietorship of any fruits in proportion to the time of his absence, and cannot, even though no other declaration follows the present one, retain them with a safe conscience, but is bound, even in his default, through his ecclesiatical superior, to apply them to the treasury of the churches or to the poor of the locality; every agreement or arrangement to which appeal is made for ill-gotten fruits, whereby the aforesaid fruits might be restored to him in whole or in part, being forbidden; any privileges whatsoever granted to any college or treasury to the contrary notwithstanding.

Absolutely the same, as regards the guilt, the loss of fruits, and the penalties, does the holy Council declare and decree with reference to inferior pastors and to all others who hold any ecclesiastical benefice having the *cura animarum*; so however, should it happen that they are absent for a reason that has first been made known to and approved by the bishop, they shall leave a due allowance of the stipend to a competent vicar to be approved by the ordinary. The permission to go away, which is to be granted in writing and gratuitously, they shall not obtain for a period longer than two months except for a grave reason. In case they shall be summoned, even though not personally, by an edict, and should be contumacious, the ordinaries shall be at liberty to constrain them by ecclesiastical censures, by the sequestration and withdrawal of fruits and other legal means, even deprivation; and no privilege whatsoever, no concession, domestic position, exemption, not even by reason of some benefice, no contract or statute, even though confirmed by oath or by any authority whatsoever, no custom, even though immemorial, which is to be regarded rather as a corruption, no appeal or inhibition, even in the Roman Curia or by virtue of the constitution of Eugene, shall be able to suspend the execution hereof.

Finally, the holy Council commands that both the decree under Paul III and this present one be published in the provincial and episcopal councils; for it desires that things which so intimately concern the office of pastors and the salvation of souls be frequently impressed on the ears and mind of all, so that with the help of God they may not hereafter fall into decay either through the corrosive action of time or the forgetfulness of men or by desuetude.

CHAPTER II

THOSE PLACED OVER CHURCHES SHALL RECEIVE CONSECRATION WITHIN THREE MONTHS; WHERE THE CONSECRATION IS TO TAKE PLACE

If those who, under whatever name or title, even though they be cardinals of the holy Roman Church, have been placed over cathedral or superior churches shall not within three months have received consecration, they shall be bound to restore the fruits received; if for three more months they shall have neglected to do this, they shall be *ipso jure* deprived of their churches. Their consecration, if performed outside the Roman Curia, shall take place in the church to which they have been promoted, or in the province if it can be conveniently done.

CHAPTER III

BISHOPS, EXCEPT IN CASE OF ILLNESS, SHALL CONFER ORDERS IN PERSON

Bishops shall confer orders themselves; but should they be prevented by illness, they shall not send their subjects to another bishop to be ordained unless they have first been examined and approved.

CHAPTER IV

WHO MAY RECEIVE THE FIRST TONSURE

No one shall be admitted to the first tonsure who has not received the sacrament of confirmation; who has not been taught the rudiments of the faith; who does not know how to read and write, and concerning whom there is not a probable conjecture that he has chosen this manner of life that he may render to God a faithful service and not to escape fraudulently from civil justice.

CHAPTER V

WHEREWITH THOSE TO BE ORDAINED ARE TO BE PROVIDED

Those who are to be promoted to minor orders shall have a good testimonial from their pastor and from the master of the school in which they are educated. Those, however, who are to be raised to any one of the major orders shall a month before the ordination repair to the bishop, who shall commission the pastor, or another person whom he may deem more suitable, to make known publicly in the church the names and desire of those who wish to be promoted, to inform himself diligently from trustworthy sources regarding the birth, age, morals, and life of those to be ordained, and to transmit to the bishop as soon as possible testimonial letters containing the results of the inquiry.

CHAPTER VI

THE AGE OF FOURTEEN YEARS IS REQUIRED FOR AN ECCLESIASTICAL BENEFICE; WHO IS TO ENJOY THE *PRIVILEGIUM FORI*

No one who has received the first tonsure or is constituted in minor orders shall be able to hold a benefice before his fourteenth year. Furthermore, he shall not enjoy the *privilegium fori* unless he has an ecclesiastical benefice, or, wearing the clerical garb and tonsure, serves in some church by order of the bishop, or is in an ecclesiastical seminary or with the permission of the bishop in some school or university on the way, as it were, to the reception of major orders. As regards married clerics, the constitution of Boniface VIII, which begins, "Clerici, qui cum unicis," shall be observed, provided these clerics, being assigned by the bishop to the service or ministry of some church, serve or minister in that church and wear the clerical garb and tonsure; privilege or custom, even immemorial, shall avail no one in this matter.

CHAPTER VII

THOSE TO BE ORDAINED ARE TO BE EXAMINED BY MEN SKILLED IN DIVINE AND HUMAN LAW

The holy Council, following the footsteps of the ancient canons, decrees that when the bishop has arranged to hold an ordination, all who wish to dedicate themselves to the sacred ministry shall be summoned to the city for the Wednesday before the ordination, or any other day which the bishop may deem convenient. And calling to his assistance priests and other prudent men skilled in the divine law and experienced in the laws of the Church, the bishop shall carefully investigate and examine the parentage, person, age, education, morals, learning, and faith of those who are to be ordained.

CHAPTER VIII

HOW AND BY WHOM EACH ONE OUGHT TO BE ORDAINED

The conferring of sacred orders shall be celebrated publicly, at the times specified by law, and in the cathedral church in the presence of the canons of the church, who are to be summoned for that purpose; but if celebrated in another place of the diocese, in the presence of the local clergy, the church holding the highest rank should always, as far as possible, be chosen. Each one shall be ordained by his own bishop. But if anyone should ask to be promoted by another, this shall under no condition, even under the pretext of any general or special rescript or privilege, even at the times specified, be permitted him unless his probity and morals be recommended by the testimony of his ordinary. Otherwise the one ordaining shall be suspended for a year from conferring orders, and the one ordained shall be suspended from exercising the orders received for as long a period as his ordinary shall see fit.

CHAPTER IX

A BISHOP ORDAINING ONE OF HIS OWN HOUSEHOLD SHALL AT ONCE AND IN REALITY CONFER ON HIM A BENEFICE

A bishop may not ordain one of his household who is not his subject, unless he has lived with him for a period of three years and to the exclusion of fraud confers on him at once a benefice; any custom, even though immemorial, to the contrary notwithstanding.

Chapter X

PRELATES INFERIOR TO BISHOPS SHALL NOT CONFER THE TONSURE OR MINOR ORDERS EXCEPT ON RELIGIOUS SUBJECT TO THEM; NEITHER THEY NOR ANY CHAPTER WHATSOEVER SHALL GRANT DIMISSORY LETTERS; A SEVERER PENALTY IS PRESCRIBED AGAINST THOSE WHO TRANSGRESS THE DECREE

It shall not be lawful in the future for abbots and any other persons, however exempt, residing within the limits of a diocese, even in case they are said to be of no diocese or exempt, to confer the tonsure or minor orders on anyone who is not a religious subject to them; nor shall abbots themselves and other exempt persons, or any colleges or chapters, even those of cathedral churches, grant dimissory letters to any secular clerics that they may be ordained by others. But the ordination of all these persons, when everything contained in the decrees of this holy Council has been observed, shall pertain to the bishops within the limits of whose diocese they are; any privileges, prescriptions, or customs, even though immemorial, notwithstanding. It commands also that the penalty imposed on those who, contrary to the decree of this holy Council under Paul III, procure dimissory letters from the chapter during the vacancy of the episcopal see be extended to those who shall obtain the said letters from the chapter but from any other persons who during the vacancy of the see succeed to the jurisdiction of the bishop in lieu of the chapter. Those who issue dimissory letters contrary to the form of this decree shall be *ipso jure* suspended from their office and benefices for one year.

Chapter XI

THE INTERSTICES AND CERTAIN OTHER REGULATIONS TO BE OBSERVED IN THE RECEPTION OF MINOR ORDERS

The minor orders shall be conferred on those who understand at least the Latin language, observing the prescribed interstices, unless the bishop should deem it more expedient to act otherwise, that they may be taught more accurately how great is the burden of this vocation and may in accordance with the direction of the bishop exercise themselves in each office, and this in the church to which they will be assigned (unless they happen to be absent *causa studiorum*); and thus they shall ascend step by step, that with increasing age they may grow in worthiness of life and in learning, which especially the example of their good conduct, their assiduous service in the Church, their greater reverence toward priests and the superior orders, and a more frequent communion than heretofore of the body of Christ will prove. And since from here there is entrance to the higher orders and to the most sacred mysteries, no one shall be admitted to them whom the promise of knowledge does not show to be worthy of the major orders. These, however, shall not be promoted to sacred orders till a year after the reception of the last of the minor orders, unless necessity or the need of the Church shall in the judgment of the bishop require otherwise.

Chapter XII

THE AGE REQUIRED FOR MAJOR ORDERS; ONLY THOSE WORTHY ARE TO BE ADMITTED

No one shall in the future be promoted to the subdiaconate before the twenty-second, to the diaconate before the twenty-third, and to the priesthood before the twenty-fifth year of his age. However, the bishops should know that not all who have attained that age are to be admitted to these orders, but those only who are worthy and whose upright life is as old age. Regulars likewise shall not be ordained below that age or without a careful examination by the bishop; all privileges whatsoever in this respect being completely set aside.

Chapter XIII

WHO MAY BE ORDAINED SUBDEACON AND DEACON; THEIR OBLIGATIONS; ON NO ONE SHALL TWO SACRED ORDERS BE CONFERRED THE SAME DAY

Those shall be ordained subdeacons and deacons who have a good testimonial [see 1 Tim. 3:7], have already been approved in minor orders, and are instructed in letters and in those things that pertain to the exercise of the orders. They should hope, with the help of God, to be able to live continently, should serve the churches to which they will be assigned, understand that it is very highly becoming, since they serve at the altar, to receive holy communion at least on the Lord's days and on solemn festival days. Those who have been promoted to the sacred order of subdeacon shall not till they have completed at least one year therein be permitted to ascend to a higher order, unless the bishop shall judge otherwise. Two sacred orders shall not be conferred on the same day, even to regulars, any privileges and indults whatsoever to whomsoever granted to the contrary notwithstanding.

CHAPTER XIV

WHO ARE TO BE PROMOTED TO THE PRIESTHOOD; THE OFFICE OF THOSE SO PROMOTED

Those who have conducted themselves piously and faithfully in their performance of earlier functions and are accepted for the order of priesthood, shall have a good testimonial [cf. 1 Tim. 3:7] and be persons who not only have served in the office of deacon for one entire year, unless by reason of the advantage and need of the Church the bishop should judge otherwise, but who also by a previous careful examination have been found competent to teach the people those things which are necessary for all to know unto salvation, and competent also to administer the sacraments, and so conspicuous for piety and purity of morals that a shining example of good works and a guidance for good living may be expected from them. The bishop shall see to it that they celebrate Mass at least on the Lord's days and on solemn festivals, but if they have the *cura animarum*, as often as their duty requires. To those who have been promoted *per saltum,* the bishop may for a legitimate reason grant a dispensation, provided they have not exercised the ministry.

CHAPTER XV

NO ONE SHALL HEAR CONFESSIONS UNLESS APPROVED BY THE ORDINARY

Although priests receive by ordination the power of absolving from sins, nevertheless the holy Council decrees that no one, even though a regular, can hear the confessions of seculars, even priests, and that he is not to be regarded as qualified thereto, unless he either holds a parochial benefice or is by the bishops, after an examination, if they should deem it necessary, or in some other manner, judged competent and has obtained their approval, which shall be given gratuitously; any privileges and custom whatsoever, even immemorial, notwithstanding.

Chapter XVI

VAGRANTS AND PERSONS USELESS TO THE CHURCHES SHALL BE EXCLUDED FROM ORDERS

Since no one ought to be ordained who in the judgment of his bishop is not useful or necessary to his churches, the holy Council, following the footsteps of the sixth canon of the Council of Chalcedon, decrees that no one shall in the future be ordained who is not assigned to that church or pious place for the need or utility of which he is promoted, where he may discharge his duties and not wander about without any fixed abode. But if he shall desert that place without consulting the bishop, he shall be forbidden the exercise of the sacred orders. Furthermore, no cleric who is a stranger shall, without commendatory letters from his ordinary, be admitted by any bishop to celebrate the divine mysteries and to administer the sacraments.

Chapter XVII

IN WHAT MANNER THE EXERCISE OF THE MINOR ORDERS IS TO BE RESTORED

That the functions of holy orders from the deacon to the porter, which have been laudably received in the Church from the times of the Apostles, and which have been for some time discontinued in many localities, may again be restored to use in accordance with the canons, and may not be derided by the heretics as useless, the holy Council, burning with the desire to restore the ancient usage, decrees that in the future such functions shall not be exercised except by those constituted in these orders, and it exhorts in the Lord each and all prelates of the churches and commands them that they make it their care to restore these functions, as far as it can be conveniently done, in cathedral, collegiate, and parochial churches of their diocese if the number of people and the revenues of the church are able to bear it. To those exercising these functions they shall assign salaries from a part of the revenues of some simple benefices or of the church treasury if the revenues are adequate, or from the revenues of both, and of these salaries they may, if they prove negligent, be deprived in whole or in part by the judgment of the bishop. In case there should not be at hand unmarried clerics to exercise the functions of the four minor orders, their place may be supplied by married clerics of approved life, provided they have not married a second time, are competent to discharge the duties, and wear the tonsure and the clerical garb in church.

CHAPTER XVIII

DIRECTIONS FOR ESTABLISHING SEMINARIES FOR CLERICS, ESPECIALLY THE YOUNGER ONES; IN THEIR ERECTION MANY THINGS ARE TO BE OBSERVED; THE EDUCATION OF THOSE TO BE PROMOTED TO CATHEDRAL AND MAJOR CHURCHES

Since the age of youth, unless rightly trained, is inclined to follow after the pleasure of the world, and unless educated from its tender years in piety and religion before the habits of vice take possession of the whole man, will never perfectly and without the greatest and well-nigh extraordinary help of Almighty God persevere in ecclesiastical discipline, the holy Council decrees that all cathedral and metropolitan churches and churches greater than these shall be bound, each according to its means and the extent of its diocese, to provide for, to educate in religion, and to train in ecclesiastical discipline, a certain number of boys of their city and diocese, or, if they are not found there, of their province, in a college located near the said churches or in some other suitable place to be chosen by the bishop. Into this college shall be received such as are at least twelve years of age, are born of lawful wedlock, who know how to read and write competently, and whose character and inclination justify the hope that they will dedicate themselves forever to the ecclesiastical ministry. It wishes, however, that in the selection the sons of the poor be given preference, though it does not exclude those of the wealthy class, provided they be maintained at their own expense and manifest a zeal to serve God and the Church. These youths the bishop shall divide into as many classes as he may deem proper, according to their number, age, and progress in ecclesiastical discipline, and shall, when it appears to him opportune, assign some of them to the ministry of the churches, the others he shall keep in the college to be instructed, and he shall replace by others those who have been withdrawn, so that the college may be a perpetual seminary of ministers of God. And that they may be the better trained in the aforesaid ecclesiastical discipline, they shall forthwith and always wear the tonsure and the clerical garb; they shall study grammar, singing, ecclesiastical computation, and other useful arts; shall be instructed in Sacred Scripture, ecclesiastical books, the homilies of the saints, the manner of administering the sacraments, especially those things that seem adapted to the hearing of confessions, and the rites and ceremonies. The bishop shall see to it that they are present every day at the sacrifice of the Mass, confess their sins at least once a month, receive the body of our Lord Jesus Christ in accordance with the directions of their confessor, and on festival days serve in the cathedral and other churches of the locality. All these and other things beneficial and needful for this purpose each bishop shall prescribe with the advice of two of the senior and more reputable canons chosen by himself as the Holy Ghost shall suggest, and they shall make it their duty by frequent visitation to see to it that they are always observed. The disobedient and incorrigible, and the disseminators of depraved morals they shall punish severely, even with expulsion if necessary; and removing all obstacles, they shall foster carefully whatever appears to contribute to the advancement and preservation of so pious and holy an institution. And since for the construction of the college, for paying salaries to instructors and servants, for the maintenance of the youths and for other expenses, certain revenues will be necessary, the bishops shall, apart from those funds which are in some churches and localities set aside for the instruction and maintenance of youths, and which are *eo ipso* to be considered as applied to this seminary under the care of the bishop, with the advice of two of the chapter, of whom one shall be chosen by the bishop, the other by the chapter, and also of two of the clergy of the city, the choice of one of whom shall in like manner be with the bishop, the other with the clergy, deduct a certain part or portion from the entire revenues of the bishop and of the chapter, and of all dignities with and without jurisdiction, offices, prebends, portions, abbeys, and priories of whatever order, even though regular, whatever their character and rank; also of hospitals which, according to the constitution of the Council of Vienne, which begins "Quia contingit," are conferred as title or with a view of administration; also of all benefices, even those of regulars, though they enjoy the right of patronage, even if exempt, or belong to no diocese, or are annexed to other churches, monasteries, hospitals, or to any other pious places even though exempt; also of the treasuries of the churches and of other places, and of all other ecclesiastical revenues or incomes, even those of other colleges (in which, however, the seminaries of students and instructors promoting the common good of the Church are not actually included, for the Council wishes these to be exempt, except with reference to such revenues as exceed the expense of the suitable maintenance of these seminaries), or associations or confraternities, which in some localities are called schools; and of all monasteries, except those of the mendicants; also of all tithes belonging in any way to laics, from which ecclesiastical maintenance is customarily paid, and of those also which belong to knights, of whatever military body or order they may be, the brethren of St. John of Jerusalem alone excepted; and the part or portion so deducted, as also some simple benefices, of whatever nature or rank, and prestimonies, or prestimonial portions as they are called, even before they become vacant, without prejudice, however, to the divine service or to those who hold them, they shall apply to and incorporate in this college. This shall have effect whether the benefices be reserved or assigned; and the unions and assignments of these benefices can be neither suspended through resignation nor in any way hindered, but they shall have their effect, any vacancy, even in the Curia, notwithstanding, or any constitution whatsoever. For the payment of this portion the local bishop shall by ecclesiastical censures and other legal means, even with the aid of the secular arm, should he deem it necessary, compel the possessors of benefices, dignities with and without jurisdiction, and each and all of the above-mentioned, whether the revenues are for themselves or for the salaries which they perchance pay to others out of the said revenues, retaining, however, a portion equivalent to that which they have to pay on account of these salaries; any privileges, exemptions, even such as might require a special declaration of annulment, custom, even though immemorial, any appeal and allegation which might hinder the execution of any or all of the above, notwithstanding. But if it should happen that as a result of these unions or otherwise, the seminary should be found to be endowed in whole or in part, then the portion deducted from each benefice, as stated above, and incorporated by the bishop, shall be discontinued in whole or in part as circumstances may require. And if the prelates of cathedrals and other major churches should prove negligent in the erection of the seminary and its maintenance and should decline to pay their portion, it shall be the duty of the archbishop to rebuke the bishop sharply and compel him to comply with all the aforesaid matters, and of the provincial synod to rebuke sharply and compel in like manner the archbishop and superiors, and diligently to see to it that this holy and pious work be, wherever possible, expedited without delay. The bishop shall receive annually the accounts of the revenues of the seminary in the presence of two delegated by the chapter and of as many delegated by the clergy of the city.

Furthermore, in order that the establishment of schools of this kind may be procured at less expense, the holy Council decrees that bishops, archbishops, primates, and other local ordinaries urge and compel, even by the reduction of their revenues, those who hold the position of instructor and others to whose position is attached the function of reading or teaching to teach those to be educated in those schools personally, if they are competent, otherwise by competent substitutes, to be chosen by themselves and to be approved by the ordinaries. But if these in the judgment of the bishop are not qualified, they shall choose another who is competent, no appeal being permitted; and should they neglect to do this, then the bishop himself shall appoint one. The aforesaid instructors shall teach what the bishop shall judge expedient. In the future, however, those offices or dignities, which are called professorships, shall not be conferred except on doctors or masters or licentiates of Sacred Scripture or canon law and on other competent persons who can personally discharge that office; any appointment made otherwise shall be null and void, all privileges and customs whatsoever, even though immemorial, notwithstanding.

But if in any province the churches labor under such poverty that in some a college cannot be established, then the provincial synod or the metropolitan with two of the oldest suffragans shall provide for the establishment of one or more colleges, as he may deem advisable, at the metropolitan or at some other more convenient church of the province, from the revenues of two or more churches in each of which a college cannot be conveniently established, where the youths of those churches might be educated. In churches having extensive dioceses, however, the bishop may have one or more in the diocese, as he may deem expedient; which, however, shall in all things be dependent on the one erected and established in the [metropolitan] city.

Finally, if with regard to either the unions or the appraisement or assignment or incorporation of portions, or for any other reason, any difficulty should happen to arise by reason of which the establishment or the maintenance of the seminary might be hindered or disturbed, the bishop with those designated above or the provincial synod shall have the authority, according to the custom of the country and the character of the churches and benefices, to decide and regulate all matters which shall appear necessary and expedient for the happy advancement of the seminary, even to modify or augment, if need be, the contents hereof.

Decree of the Twenty-Fourth Session

CHAPTER I

NORMS OF PROCEDURE IN THE ELECTION OF
BISHOPS AND CARDINALS

If in all ecclesiastical grades a prudent and enlightened attention is necessary in order that in the house of the Lord there be nothing disorderly and nothing unbecoming, much more ought we to strive that no error be committed in the election of him who is constituted above all grades. For the state and order of the entire household of the Lord will totter if what is required in the body be not found in the head. Hence, although the holy Council has elsewhere decided to advantage a number of things concerning those to be promoted to cathedral and major churches, yet it considers this office to be of such a nature that if viewed in its greatness, there can never be caution enough taken concerning it. Wherefore it decrees that as soon as a church becomes vacant, public and private supplications and prayers be made and be ordered throughout the city and diocese by the chapter, that clergy and people may implore God for a good shepherd. It moreover exhorts and admonishes each and all who in any manner have a right from the Apostolic See to participate in the promotion of those to be placed in authority, or who otherwise render assistance (due to the circumstances of the present time no change being made herein), that they above all bear in mind that they can do nothing more serviceable to the glory of God and the salvation of the people than to exert themselves to the end that good and competent shepherds be promoted to the government of the Church, and that they become partakers in the sins of others and sin mortally unless they strive diligently that those be promoted

whom they judge the more worthy and useful to the Church, not
moved by entreaties or human affection, or the solicitations of
rivals, but because their merits speak for them, whom they know
to be persons of lawful wedlock, and whose life, age, learning,
and all other qualifications meet the requirements of the sacred
canons and the decrees of this Council of Trent. But since the
taking of the important and competent testimony of upright and
learned men regarding the aforesaid qualifications cannot by reason of the diversity of nations, peoples, and customs be everywhere uniformly followed, the holy Council commands that in
the provincial synod to be held by the metropolitan, there be
prescribed for each place and province a special or proper form of
the examination, investigation, or instruction to be made, such as
shall appear most useful and suitable for these places and which is
to be submitted to the approval of the most holy Roman pontiff;
so however that, after the completion of the examination or
investigation of the person to be promoted, it shall, after having
been put in the form of a public document, be transmitted as soon
as possible, with all the attestations and with the profession of
faith made by the one to be promoted, to the most holy Roman
pontiff, in order that the Roman pontiff himself, with a complete
knowledge of the whole matter and of the persons before him,
may for the benefit of the Lord's flock provide the churches more
profitably if in the examination or investigation they have been
found competent. All examinations, investigations, attestations,
and proofs of whatever kind and by whomever made, even though
in the Roman Curia, concerning the qualifications of the one to
be promoted and the condition of the church, shall be carefully
examined by the cardinal, who shall report thereon to the consistory, and three other cardinals; and this report shall be authenti-
cated by the signature of the cardinal making the report and of the
three other cardinals, in which each of the four cardinals shall
affirm that, after having given it his careful attention, he has found
those to be promoted to possess the qualifications required by law
and by this holy Council and at the peril of his eternal salvation
firmly believes that they are competent to be placed over churches;
and the report having been made in one consistory, that the
investigation may in the meantime receive more mature consideration, the decision shall be deferred to another consistory, unless

the most blessed pontiff shall deem it expedient to act otherwise. Each and all of the particulars relative to the life, age, learning, and the other qualifications of those who are to be appointed bishops, which have been determined elsewhere by this Council, the same it decrees are to be required in the election of the cardinals of the holy Roman Church, even though they be deacons, whom the most holy Roman pontiff shall, insofar as it can be conveniently done, choose from all the nations of Christendom according as he finds them competent. Finally, the same holy council, moved by so many very grave afflictions of the Church, cannot but call to mind that nothing is more necessary to the Church of God than that the holy Roman pontiff apply that solicitude which by the duty of his office he owes the universal Church in a very special way by associating with himself as cardinals the most select persons only, and appoint to each church most eminently upright and competent shepherds; and this the more so, because our Lord Jesus Christ will require at his hands the blood of the sheep of Christ that perish through the evil government of shepherds who are negligent and forgetful of their office.

CHAPTER II

PROVINCIAL SYNODS ARE TO BE CELEBRATED EVERY THREE YEARS, DIOCESAN SYNODS EVERY YEAR; WHO ARE TO CONVOKE THEM AND WHO ARE TO BE PRESENT THEREAT

Provincial synods, wherever they have been omitted, shall be restored for the regulation of morals, the correction of abuses, the settlement of controversies, and for other purposes permitted by the sacred canons. Wherefore the metropolitans in person, or if they are legitimately hindered, the oldest suffragan bishop, shall not neglect to convoke, each in his own province, a synod within a year at least from the termination of the present council and after that at least every third year, after the octave of the resurrection of our Lord Jesus Christ or at some other more convenient time, according to the custom of the province, which all the bishops and others who by right or custom are under obligation to be present shall be absolutely bound to attend, those being excepted who at imminent danger would have to cross the sea. The bishops of the province shall not in the future be compelled under pretext of any custom whatsoever to go against their will to the metropolitan church. Those bishops likewise who are not subject to any archbishop shall once for all choose some neighboring metropolitan, at whose provincial synod they shall be obliged to be present with the other bishops, and whatever has been decided therein they shall observe and cause to be observed. In all other respects their exemption and privileges shall remain intact and entire. Diocesan synods also are to be celebrated annually; at which also all those exempt, who would otherwise by reason of the cessation of that exemption have to attend and who are not subject to general chapters, shall be bound to assemble, those also who have charge of parochial or other secular churches, even though annexed, whoever they may be, must be present at the synod. But if the metropolitans and also the bishops and the others mentioned above prove negligent in these matters, they shall incur the penalties prescribed by the sacred canons.

CHAPTER III

IN WHAT MANNER PRELATES ARE TO MAKE THEIR VISITATION

Patriarchs, primates, metropolitans and bishops shall not neglect to visit their respective dioceses, either personally or, if they are lawfully hindered, through their vicar-general or visitor; if by reason of its extent they are unable to make a visitation of the whole annually, they shall either themselves or through their visitors visit at least the greater part of it, so that the whole may be completed in two years. Metropolitans, even after a complete visitation of their own diocese, shall not visit the cathedral churches or the dioceses of the bishops of their province, except for a cause taken cognizance of and approved by the provincial synod. Archdeacons, deans, and other inferiors shall visit those churches in which they have thus far been accustomed legally to make visitations, but from now on with the consent of the bishop personally and with the aid of a notary. Also the visitors delegated by a chapter, where the chapter has the right of visitation, shall be first approved by the bishop; thereby, however, the bishop, or if he be hindered, his visitor, shall not be prohibited from visiting those same churches apart from these, and the archdeacons and other inferiors shall be bound to render to him an account within a month of the visitation made by them, and to show him the depositions of witnesses and the entire proceedings; any custom, even though immemorial, and any exemptions and privileges whatsoever notwithstanding. But the chief purpose of all these visitations shall be, after the extirpation of heresies, to restore sound and orthodox doctrine, to guard good morals and to correct such as are evil, to animate the people by exhortations and admonitions with religion, peace, and innocence, and to regulate the rest for the benefit of the faithful as the prudence of the visitors may suggest, allowance being made for place, time, and occasion. That these things may be more easily and happily accomplished, each and all of the aforesaid to whom the right of visitation belongs are admonished to treat all with a fatherly love and Christian zeal; and therefore content with a modest train of horses and servants, let them strive to complete the visitation as speedily as possible, yet with due attention. Meanwhile they shall exercise care that they do not become troublesome or a burden to anyone by useless expenses, and neither shall they nor any one of theirs, either by way of compensation for the visitation or from wills made for pious purposes, except what is by right due to them from pious bequests, or under any other name, receive anything, be it money or gift of whatever kind or in whatever way offered, any custom, even though immemorial, notwithstanding; with the exception, however, of food, which shall be furnished them and theirs frugally and in moderation during the time necessary for the visitation only and not beyond that. It shall, however, be left to the option of those who are visited to pay, if they prefer, what in accordance with a fixed assessment they have been accustomed to pay in money heretofore, or to furnish the food; inviolate also shall remain the right of old agreements entered into with monasteries or other pious places or with churches not parochial. But in those places or provinces where it is the custom that neither food nor money or anything else be received by the visitors, but that all be done gratuitously, that practice shall continue there. But if anyone, which God forbid, shall presume to receive more in any of the cases mentioned above, in addition to the restitution of double the amount to be made within a month, he shall also incur without hope of pardon the other penalties contained in the constitution of the General Council of Lyons, which begins "Exigit," as well as those of the provincial synod at the discretion of that synod. Patrons shall not presume in any way to intrude themselves in those things that pertain to the administration of the sacraments; they shall not interfere with the visitation of the ornaments of the church, or its immovable properties, or the revenues of the buildings, except insofar as they are competent to do this by reason of the institution and foundation; but the bishops themselves shall attend to these things and shall see to it that the revenues of the buildings are devoted to purposes necessary and useful to the Church according as they shall deem most expedient.

CHAPTER IV

BY WHOM AND WHEN THE OFFICE OF PREACHING IS TO BE DISCHARGED. THE PARISH CHURCH IS TO BE ATTENDED TO HEAR THE WORD OF GOD. NO ONE MAY PREACH WITHOUT THE PERMISSION OF THE BISHOP

Desiring that the office of preaching, which belongs chiefly to bishops, be exercised as often as possible for the welfare of the faithful, the holy Council, for the purpose of accommodating to the use of the present time the canons published elsewhere on this subject under Paul III, of happy memory, decrees that they themselves shall personally, each in his own church, announce the Sacred Scriptures and the divine law, or, if lawfully hindered, have it done by those whom they shall appoint to the office of preaching; but in other churches by the parish priests, or, if they are hindered, by others to be appointed by the bishop in the city or in any part of the diocese as they shall judge it expedient, at the expense of those who are bound or accustomed to defray it, and this they shall do at least on all Sundays and solemn festival days, but during the season of fasts, of Lent and of the Advent of the Lord, daily, or at least on three days of the week if they shall deem it necessary; otherwise, as often as they shall judge that it can be done conveniently. The bishop shall diligently admonish the people that each one is bound to be present at his own parish church, where it can be conveniently done, to hear the word of God. But no one, whether secular or regular, shall presume to preach, even in churches of his own order, in opposition to the will of the bishop. The bishops shall also see to it that at least on Sundays and other festival days, the children in every parish be carefully taught the rudiments of the faith and obedience toward God and their parents by those whose duty it is, and who shall be compelled thereto, if need be, even by ecclesiastical censures; any privileges and customs notwithstanding. In other respects the things decreed under Paul III concerning the office of preaching shall remain in force.

CHAPTER V

MAJOR CRIMINAL CAUSES AGAINST BISHOPS SHALL BE TAKEN COGNIZANCE OF BY THE SUPREME PONTIFF ONLY, MINOR ONES BY THE PROVINCIAL SYNOD

Graver criminal causes against bishops, also that of heresy, which may God prevent, which merit deposition or deprivation, shall be taken cognizance of and decided by the Roman pontiff only. But if the cause be of such a nature that it must perforce be assigned out of the Roman Curia, it shall not be committed to anyone but metropolitans or bishops to be chosen by the most holy pope. This commission shall be both special and signed by the most holy pontiff's own hand, and he shall never grant more to them than this, that they take information only of the fact and draw up the process, which they shall transmit immediately to the Roman pontiff, the definitive sentence being reserved to His Holiness. The other things decreed elsewhere under Julius III, of happy memory, concerning these matters, as also the constitution of the general council under Innocent III, which begins, "Qualiter et quando," and which the holy Council renews in the present decree, shall be observed by all. But the minor criminal causes of bishops shall be taken cognizance of and decided in the provincial synod only, or by persons commissioned by the provincial synod.

CHAPTER VI

AUTHORITY IS GIVEN TO THE BISHOPS TO DISPENSE IN CASES OF IRREGULARITY AND SUSPENSION AND TO ABSOLVE FROM CRIMES

Bishops are authorized to dispense in all cases of irregularity and suspension resulting from a secret crime, except that arising from willful homicide and those arising from crimes that have found their way before a tribunal, and to absolve gratuitously, after the imposition of a salutary penance, *per se* or through a vicar especially appointed for this purpose *in foro conscientiae* in all occult cases, even those reserved to the Apostolic See, all delinquents subject to them in their diocese. The same is permitted them only, but not their vicars, in the same forum with respect to the crime of heresy.

CHAPTER VII

THE EFFICACY OF THE SACRAMENTS SHALL BE EXPLAINED BY BISHOPS AND PARISH PRIESTS BEFORE THEY ARE ADMINISTERED TO THE PEOPLE. DURING THE CELEBRATION OF THE MASS THE SACRED SCRIPTURES ARE TO BE EXPLAINED

That the faithful may approach the sacraments with greater reverence and devotion of mind, the holy Council commands all bishops that not only when they themselves are about to administer them to the people, they shall first, in a manner adapted to the mental ability of those who receive them, explain their efficacy and use, but also that they shall see to it that the same is done piously and prudently by every parish priest, and in the vernacular tongue, if need be and if it can be done conveniently, in accordance with the form which will be prescribed for each of the sacraments by the holy Council in a catechism, which the bishops shall have faithfully translated into the language of the people and explained to the people by all parish priests. In like manner shall they explain on all festivals or solemnities during the solemnization of the Mass or the celebration of the divine offices, in the vernacular tongue, the divine commands and the maxims of salvation, and leaving aside useless questions, let them strive to engraft these things on the hearts of all and instruct them in the law of the Lord.

CHAPTER VIII

PUBLIC SINNERS SHALL DO PUBLIC PENANCE, UNLESS THE BISHOP SHALL DETERMINE OTHERWISE; A PENITENTIARY IS TO BE INSTITUTED IN CATHEDRALS

The Apostle admonishes that those who sin publicly are to be reproved publicly [see 1 Tim. 5:20]. When therefore anyone has publicly and in the sight of many committed a crime by which there is no doubt that others have been offended and scandalized, it is proper that a penance commensurate with his guilt be publicly imposed on him, so that those whom he by his example has led to evil morals, he may bring back to an upright life by the evidence of his correction. The bishop, however, should he judge it advisable, may commute this kind of public penance to one that is secret. In all cathedral churches where it can be conveniently done, let the bishop appoint a penitentiary united with the prebend that shall next become vacant, who shall be a master or doctor or licentiate in theology or canon law and forty years of age, or another who may be found to be more suitable for the character of the place and who, while he is hearing confessions in the church, shall be considered as present in the choir.

CHAPTER IX

BY WHOM THOSE SECULAR CHURCHES ARE TO BE VISITED THAT BELONG TO NO DIOCESE

What has elsewhere been ordained by this council under Paul III, of happy memory, and lately under our most blessed Lord Pius IV, regarding the attention to be given by ordinaries to the visitation of benefices, even of those exempt, the same is to be observed also with regard to those secular churches which are said to be in no one's diocese, namely, that they be visited by the bishop whose cathedral church is the nearest, if that is agreed upon, otherwise by him, acting as delegate of the Apostolic See, who has once been chosen for this in the provincial synod by the prelate of that place; any privileges and customs whatsoever, even though immemorial, notwithstanding.

CHAPTER X

THE EXECUTION OF THE VISITATION SHALL NOT BE IMPEDED BY THE SUBJECTS

That the bishops may be better able to keep the people whom they rule in duty and obedience, they shall in all those things that concern visitation and the correction of the morals of their subjects have the right and authority, also as delegates of the Apostolic See, to decree, regulate, punish, and execute, in accordance with the prescriptions of the canons, those things which in their prudence shall appear to them necessary for the emendation of their subjects and for the good of their dioceses. And in these matters, where it is question of visitation and correction of morals, no exemption, inhibition, appeal or complaint, even though submitted to the Apostolic See, shall in any manner whatsoever hinder or suspend the execution of those things which shall have been commanded, decreed, or adjudicated by them.

CHAPTER XI

HONORARY TITLES OR SPECIAL PRIVILEGES SHALL NOT DETRACT IN ANY WAY FROM THE RIGHT OF BISHOPS. THE CHAPTER "CUM CAPELLA," CONCERNING PRIVILEGES, IS RENEWED

Since privileges and exemptions which are granted to many persons under various titles are known to create confusion nowadays in the jurisdiction of bishops and to give to those exempt occasion for a more unrestrained life, the holy Council decrees that whenever it should be thought proper for just, weighty, and apparently necessary reasons that some persons be decorated with the honorary titles of Prothonotary, Acolyte, Count Palatine, Royal Chaplain, or other such titles of distinction, whether in or out of the Roman Curia, as also others granted to any monasteries or in any manner imparted, whether assumed under the name of servants to military orders, monasteries, hospitals, colleges, or under any other title, it is to be understood that by these privileges nothing is taken away from the ordinaries whereby those persons to whom such privileges have already been granted or to whom they may be granted in the future cease to be fully subject in all things to the ordinaries as delegates of the Apostolic See; and as regards Royal Chaplains, let them be subject in accordance with the constitution of Innocent III, which begins, "Cum capella"; those persons, however, being excepted who are engaged in actual service in the aforesaid places or in military orders and who reside within their enclosures or houses and live under obedience to them, and those also who have lawfully and according to the rule of these military orders made profession, whereof the ordinary must be certified; notwithstanding any privileges whatsoever, even those of the order of St. John of Jerusalem and of other military orders. But those privileges which by virtue of the constitution of Eugene they are accustomed to enjoy who reside in the Roman Curia or who are in the household of cardinals are by no means to be understood as applying to those who hold ecclesiastical benefices in regard to those benefices, but they shall continue to be subject to the jurisdiction of the ordinaries; any inhibitions whatsoever notwithstanding.

Chapter XII

QUALIFICATIONS NECESSARY FOR THOSE WHO ARE TO BE PROMOTED TO THE DIGNITIES AND CANONRIES OF CATHEDRAL CHURCHES AND THE DUTIES OF THOSE SO PROMOTED

Since dignities, especially in cathedral churches, were instituted to maintain and promote ecclesiastical discipline, to the end that those who hold them might be distinguished for piety, be an example to others, and assist the bishops by their labor and service, it is but right that those who are called to them should be such as are able to perform their duty. Wherefore, in the future no one shall be promoted to any dignities whatsoever to which is annexed the *cura animarum*, who has not attained at least the twenty-fifth year of his age, is experienced in the clerical order, and is recommended by the learning necessary for the discharge of his office and the integrity of his morals, comformably to the constitution of Alexander III promulgated in the Council of the Lateran, which begins, "Cum in cunctis." In like manner archdeacons, who are called the eyes of the bishop, shall in all churches where it is possible be masters in theology, or doctors or licentiates in canon law. To other dignities or offices to which no *cura animarum* is annexed, clerics, in other respects qualified, shall not be promoted unless they are twenty-two years of age. Those also who are promoted to any benefices whatever having the *cura animarum* shall within at least two months from the day of having taken possession be bound to make in the hands of the bishop, or, if he be hindered, in the presence of his vicar-general or official, a public profession of their orthodox faith and to promise solemnly and swear that they will persevere in their obedience to the Roman Church. But those who are promoted to canonries and dignities in cathedral churches shall be bound to do this not only in the presence of the bishop or his official but also in the chapter. Otherwise all those promoted as aforesaid shall not make the fruits their own; neither shall possession be of any avail to them. Furthermore, no one shall in the future be admitted to a dignity, canonry, or portion unless he is either already constituted in the sacred order which that dignity, prebend, or portion requires, or is of such an age as will qualify him for the reception of that order within the time prescribed by law and by this holy Council. In all cathedral churches all canonries and portions shall be attached to the order of the priesthood, deaconship, or subdeaconship, and the bishop shall with the advice of the chapter designate and distribute, as he shall deem expedient, to which each of the sacred orders is for the future to be attached; so however that at least one half shall be priests and the rest deacons or subdeacons. But where the more laudable custom obtains that the greater part or all shall be priests, this shall by all means be observed. The holy Council also exhorts that in provinces where it can be conveniently done all dignities and at least one half of the canonries in cathedral and prominent collegiate churches be conferred only on masters or doctors, or also on licentiates in theology or canon law. Moreover, those who hold dignities, canonries, prebends, or portions in such cathedral or collegiate churches shall not be permitted by virtue of any statute or custom to be absent from those churches more than three months of each year, saving however the statutes of those churches which require a longer period of service; otherwise every offender shall for the first year be deprived of one half of the fruits which he has made his own even by reason of his prebend and residence. But if he be again guilty of the same negligence, he shall be deprived of all the fruits which he has acquired during that year, and if he should become more contumacious, he shall be proceeded against in accordance with the prescriptions of the sacred canons. Those shall receive distributions who have been present at the appointed hours; the others shall, all collusion and remission being debarred, forfeit them in accordance with the decree of Boniface VIII, which begins "Consuetudinem," and which the holy Council restores to practice; any statutes or customs whatsoever notwithstanding. All shall be obliged to perform the divine offices in person and not by substitutes; also to assist and serve the bishop when celebrating or exercising other pontifical functions, and in the choir instituted for psalmody, to praise the name of God reverently, distinctly, and devoutly in hymns and canticles. They shall, moreover, wear at all times, both in and out of church, a becoming dress, shall abstain from unlawful hunting, fowling, dancing, taverns and games, and so excel in integrity of morals that they may with justice be called counselors of the Church. With regard to matters that pertain to the proper manner of conducting the divine offices, the proper way of singing or modulating therein, the definite rule for assembling and remaining in choir, the things necessary for those who minister in the church, and such like, the provincial synod shall prescribe for each province a fixed form that will be beneficial to and in accordance with the usage of each province. In the meantime, the bishop, with the aid of no less than two canons, one chosen by himself, the other by the chapter, may provide in these matters as he may deem expedient.

CHAPTER XIII

HOW THE POORER CATHEDRAL AND PARISH CHURCHES ARE TO BE PROVIDED FOR. PARISHES ARE TO BE SEPARATED BY DEFINITE BOUNDARIES

Since the revenues of many cathedral churches are so limited and scanty that they are in no way in keeping with the episcopal dignity and insufficient for the needs of the churches, the provincial synod, having summoned those who are concerned, shall examine and consider carefully what churches it may be advisable by reason of their limited means and poverty to unite to others in the neighborhood or to provide with additional revenues; and the completed documents concerning this matter it shall send to the supreme Roman pontiff, who being informed thereby shall, as he in his prudence may deem advisable, either unite the poorly provided churches or by additional revenues improve them. In the meantime, until the aforesaid provisions are carried into effect, the supreme pontiff may from certain benefices assist those bishops who by reason of the poverty of their diocese are in need of revenues; provided, however, these benefices are not *curae* or dignities or canonries and prebends, or monasteries in which there is regular observance, or which are subject to general chapters or to certain visitors. In parochial churches also in which the revenues are in like manner so small that they are insufficient to meet the necessary obligations, the bishop, if unable to meet the exigency by a union of benefices, not however those of regulars, shall see to it that by the assignment of first fruits or tithes or by the contributions and collections of the parishioners, or in some other way that he shall deem more profitable, as much be collected as may decently suffice for the needs of the rector and the parish. In all unions, however, whether to be made for the aforesaid or other reasons, parochial churches shall not be united to any monasteries whatsoever, or to abbeys or dignities, or prebends of a cathedral or collegiate church, or to other simple benefices, hospitals, or military orders, and those so united shall be investigated again by the ordinary in accordance with the decree elsewhere enacted by this council under Paul III, of happy memory, which is to be observed also and in like manner with regard to unions made since that time; notwithstanding whatever forms of words used therein, which shall be considered as sufficiently expressed here. Furthermore, all those cathedral churches whose revenues do not exceed in actual annual value the sum of one thousand ducats, and those parochial churches in which they do not exceed the sum of one hundred ducats, shall not in the future be burdened with taxes or reservations of revenues for this purpose. Also, in those cities and localities where the parochial churches have no definite boundaries, and whose rectors have not their own people whom they may rule but administer the sacraments indiscriminately to all who desire them, the holy Council commands the bishops that, for the greater security of the salvation of the souls committed to them, they divide the people into definite and distinct parishes and assign to each its own and permanent parish priest, who can know his people and from whom alone they may licitly receive the sacraments; or that they make other, more beneficial provisions as the conditions of the locality may require. They shall also see to it that the same is done as soon as possible in those cities and localities where there are no parish churches; any privileges and customs whatsoever, even though immemorial notwithstanding.

Chapter XIV

NO ONE SHALL BE ADMITTED TO THE POSSESSION OF A BENEFICE OR OF DISTRIBUTIONS WHEN THE DISTRIBUTION OF THE FRUITS IS NOT APPLIED TO PIOUS PURPOSES

In many churches, cathedral as well as collegiate and parochial, it is understood to be the practice, derived either from their constitutions or from evil customs, that in the election, presentation, nomination, institution, confirmation, collation, or other provision, or upon admission to the possession of a cathedral church or a benefice, of canonries or prebends, or to a portion of the revenues, or to the daily distributions, there are introduced certain conditions or deductions from the fruits, certain payments, promises, or unlawful compensations, or what in some churches is called mutual profits. Since the holy Council abhors these practices, it commands the bishops that they prohibit all things of this kind that are not applied to pious purposes and such methods of entering upon offices, which create a suspicion of simoniacal taint or sordid avarice, and that they examine carefully their statutes and customs in regard to the above matter, and retaining only what they approve as laudable, reject and abolish the rest as corrupt and scandalous. It also ordains that those who in any way act in contravention of what is contained in the present decree incur the penalties prescribed against simoniacs by the sacred canons and various constitutions of the supreme pontiffs, all of which it renews; notwithstanding any statutes, constitutions, and customs, even though immemorial and confirmed by Apostolic authority, in regard to which any deceit, fraud, and defect of intention may be investigated by the bishop as delegate of the Apostolic See.

Chapter XV

METHOD OF INCREASING THE SCANTY PREBENDS OF CATHEDRAL AND PROMINENT COLLEGIATE CHURCHES

In cathedral and prominent collegiate churches where the prebends are numerous and in relation to the daily distributions so small that they do not suffice for the decent maintenance of the rank of the canons in keeping with the character of the place and persons, the bishops may with the consent of the chapter combine them with some simple benefices, not however with those of regulars, or, if in this way it cannot be done, they may, with the consent of the patrons if the right of patronage belongs to laymen, reduce their number by suppressing some of them and apply the fruits and proceeds to the daily distributions of the remaining prebends; so however, that such a number remain as may conveniently serve for the celebration of divine service and be in keeping with the dignity of the church; any statutes and privileges, or any reservation whether general or special, or any expectation notwithstanding. The aforesaid unions or suppressions shall not be frustrated or hindered by any provisions whatsoever, not even by virtue of resignation or any other derogations or suspensions.

Chapter XVI

WHAT DUTY DEVOLVES UPON THE CHAPTER DURING THE VACANCY OF A SEE

When a see becomes vacant, the chapter shall, in those places where the duty of receiving the revenues devolves upon it, appoint one or more trustworthy and diligent stewards who shall take care of the ecclesiastical properties and revenues, of which they shall have to give an account to him whom it will concern. It shall also be strictly bound to appoint within eight days after the death of the bishop an official or vicar, or to confirm the incumbent, who shall be at least a doctor or licentiate in canon law, or otherwise as competent a person as is available. In case this is not done, the aforesaid appointment shall devolve upon the metropolitan. But if the church is a metropolitan one or one exempt and the chapter should prove negligent as was said above, then the oldest suffragan bishop in the metropolitan church and the bishop nearest the exempt church shall have the authority to appoint a competent steward and vicar. The bishop who is promoted to the vacant church shall with regard to the matters that pertain to him demand from the steward, vicar, and all other officials and administrators who were during the vacancy of the see appointed in his place by the chapter or others, even though they are members of the same chapter, an account of their office, jurisdiction, administration, or any other functions, and he shall have the authority to punish those who have been delinquent in their office or administration, even if the aforesaid officials, having turned in their accounts, should have obtained from the chapter or those delegated by it a quittance or discharge. The chapter shall also be bound to render to the bishop an account of documents belonging to the church, if any have come into its possession.

CHAPTER XVII

THE CONFERRING OF SEVERAL BENEFICES ON AND THEIR RETENTION BY ONE PERSON IS RESTRICTED

Since ecclesiastical order is upset when one cleric holds the offices of several, the sacred canons have piously provided that no one ought to be enrolled in two churches. But since many, led by the passion of ungodly covetousness, deceiving themselves, not God, are not ashamed to evade by various species of deceit what has been beneficially established and to hold several benefices at the same time, the holy Council desiring to restore discipline in the government of the churches, by the present decree, which it commands to be observed by all persons by whatever title distinguished, even though it be the dignity of the cardinalate, ordains that in the future one ecclesiastical benefice only shall be conferred on a person. If that is not sufficient to provide him on whom it is conferred with a decent livelihood, then it is permissible to confer on him another simple benefice that will afford a sufficiency, provided both do not require personal residence. These provisions shall apply not only to cathedral churches but also to all other benefices, whether secular or regular, even those held *in commendam*, of whatever title or character they may be. Those who now hold several parochial churches, or one cathedral and one parochial church shall be strictly bound, all dispensations and unions for life notwithstanding, retaining one parochial church only, or the cathedral church only, to resign the other parochial churches within a period of six months; otherwise the parochial churches and also all the benefices which they hold shall be considered *ipso jure* vacant and as such shall be freely conferred on other competent persons; neither can those who previously held them retain conscientiously the fruits after the time specified. The holy Council desires, however, that provision be made in some convenient way, as the supreme pontiff may see fit, for the necessities of those who resign.

CHAPTER XVIII

ON THE VACANCY OF A PAROCHIAL CHURCH THE BISHOP SHALL APPOINT THERETO A VICAR UNTIL HE HAS PROVIDED A PARISH PRIEST; IN WHAT MANNER AND BY WHOM THOSE APPOINTED TO PAROCHIAL CHURCHES ARE TO BE EXAMINED

It is highly desirable for the salvation of souls that they be directed by worthy and competent parish priests. That this may be accomplished more diligently and effectively, the holy Council decrees that when a parochial church becomes vacant, whether by death or resignation, also in the Curia, or in whatever other manner, it shall be the duty of the bishop immediately upon receipt of information regarding the vacancy of the church to appoint, if need be, a competent vicar to the same, with a suitable assignment, using his own judgment in the matter, of a portion of the fruits thereof, who shall discharge the duties in that church till it has been provided with a rector, even if it be said that the charge of the church belongs to the bishop himself and is administered by one or more; also in churches called patrimonial or receptive, in which it has been the custom of the bishop to assign the *cura animarum* to one or more, all of whom, it commands, are bound to the examination prescribed below, also if the parochial church be generally or specially reserved or assigned, even by virtue of an indult or privilege in favor of cardinals of the holy Roman Church, or of abbots or chapters. Moreover, the bishop and he who has the right of patronage shall within ten days, or such other term as the bishop shall prescribe, designate in the presence of those to be delegated as examiners some competent clerics who are to rule the church. Furthermore, it shall be permitted to others also who may know any who are fit for the office to make known their names, so that a careful investigation may afterward be made as to the age, morals, and sufficiency of each. But if in accordance with the custom of the country it should appear more suitable to the bishop or the provincial synod, those who wish to be examined may be summoned by a public notice. At the expiration of the time specified, all whose names have been entered shall be examined by the bishop, or, if hindered, by his vicar-general, and by other examiners who shall not be fewer than three, to whose votes, in case they are equal or distributed singly, the bishop or his vicar may add his in favor of whomsoever he shall deem most fit. At least six examiners shall be proposed annually by the bishop or his vicar in the diocesan synod, and they must prove satisfactory to it and be approved by it. Upon a vacancy occurring in any church, the bishop shall select three out of that number who shall conduct the examination with him, and on a subsequent vacancy he shall select out of the six aforesaid the same or three others whom he may prefer. These examiners shall be masters or doctors or licentiates in theology or canon law, or other clerics, whether regulars, also of the mendicant orders, or seculars, who appear most competent for the purpose; and all shall take an oath on the holy Gospels of God, that, every human consideration being set aside, they will discharge their duty faithfully. Let them take heed, however, that they do not by reason of this examination receive anything whatever either before or after; otherwise both they themselves and the givers will be guilty of the vice of simony, from which they cannot be absolved till they have resigned the benefices which they in any manner whatever possessed before this act, and they shall, moreover, be rendered disqualified to possess others in the future. In all these matters they shall be bound to render an account not only before God but also, if need be, to the provincial synod, by which, if it has been discovered that they have done anything in contravention of their duty, they can at its discretion be severely punished. On the completion of the examination they shall make known how many they have judged fit in the matter of age, morals, learning, prudence, and other qualifications suitable for ruling the vacant church, and from these the bishop shall choose him whom he shall judge the more competent, and to him and to none other shall the collation of the church be made by him to whom such collation pertains. If the church is under ecclesiastical patronage and the appointment thereto belongs to the bishop and to no one else, he whom the patron shall judge the more worthy among those approved by the examiners shall be bound to present himself to the bishop that he may be appointed by him. But when the appointment is to be made by any other than the bishop, then the bishop only shall choose the worthier among those who are worthy, and the patron shall present him to the one to whom the appointment belongs. If, however, the church is under lay patronage, the one presented by the patron must be examined, as above, by those delegated thereto, and is not to be admitted unless found competent. In all the above-mentioned cases, to no other than to one of those examined and approved by the examiners as aforesaid and in accordance with the above rules shall the church be committed, and no devolution or appeal, even to the Apostolic See or the legates, vice-legates, or nuncios of that See, or to any bishops or metropolitans, primates or patriarchs, shall hinder or suspend the execution of the report of the aforesaid examiners; otherwise the vicar whom the bishop has at his discretion already appointed for the time being to the vacant church or whom he may afterward appoint shall not be removed from the charge and administration of that church until it has been provided for, either by the appointment of the vicar himself or of some other person who has been approved and chosen as stated above. All provisions or appointments made otherwise than in accordance with the above-stated form shall be regarded as surreptitious; any exemptions, indults, privileges, anticipations, appropriations, new provisions, indults granted to any universities, also for a certain sum, and any other impediments whatsoever in contravention of this decree, notwithstanding. If, however, the revenues of said parochial churches should be so scanty as not to bear the burden of all this examination, or if no one should care to undergo the examination, or if by reason of open factions or dissensions, which are met with in some localities, more grievous quarrels and disturbances might easily be stirred up, the ordinary may omit this formality and have recourse to a private examination, if in conformity with his conscience and with the advice of the examiners he shall deem this expedient. The other things, however, are to be observed as above prescribed. If the provincial synod should judge that in the above regulations concerning the form of examination something ought to be added or omitted, it shall have the authority to do so.

Chapter XIX

MANDATES CONCERNING PROMOTION, EXPECTANCIES, AND OTHER THINGS OF THIS KIND ARE ABOLISHED

The holy Council decrees that mandates concerning promotion and favors which are called expectancies shall no longer be granted to anyone, even to colleges, universities, senators, or to any individuals whatsoever, even under the name of an indult, or for a certain sum, or under any other pretext; neither shall it be permitted to anyone to make use of those thus far granted. Neither shall mental reservations nor other favors whatsoever with regard to future vacancies, or indults respecting churches belonging to others, or monasteries, be granted to anyone, not even to cardinals of the holy Roman Church, and those hitherto granted shall be considered abolished.

Chapter XX

THE MANNER OF CONDUCTING CAUSES PERTAINING TO THE ECCLESIASTICAL FORUM IS PRESCRIBED

All causes belonging in any way whatever to the ecclesiastical forum, even if they relate to benefices, shall be taken cognizance of in the first instance before the local ordinaries only, and shall be completely terminated within at least two years from the day that the suit was instituted; otherwise, at the expiration of that term the parties, or either of them, shall be free to have recourse to superior, but otherwise competent, judges, who shall take up the cause as it then stands and shall see to it that it is terminated as soon as possible. Before that term they shall neither be committed to others nor withdrawn; any appeals introduced by the parties shall not be received by any superior judges, neither shall any assignment or restriction be issued by them except upon a definitive sentence or one having the force of such a sentence, and the grievance arising therefrom cannot be repaired by an appeal from the definitive sentence. From the above are to be excepted those causes which according to the prescriptions of the canons are to be dealt with before the Apostolic See, or which the supreme Roman pontiff shall for an urgent and reasonable cause judge advisable to assign or withdraw by a special rescript provided with the signature of His Holiness signed with his own hand. Furthermore, matrimonial and criminal causes shall not be left to the judgment of a dean, archdeacon, or other inferiors, even in the course of their visitation, but shall be reserved to the examination and jurisdiction of the bishop only (even though there should at the time be a dispute, in whatever instance it may be, between the bishop and the dean or archdeacon or other inferiors regarding the examination of those causes), and if in the same matrimonial cause one of the parties should in the presence of the bishop really prove his poverty, he shall not be compelled to litigate his case either in the second or third instance outside the province, unless the other party is prepared to provide for his maintenance and bear the expenses of the trial. In like manner, legates, also those *de latere*, nuncios, ecclesiastical governors, or others, shall not only not presume by virtue of any authority whatsoever to hinder bishops in the aforesaid causes, or in any manner take away the exercise of or disturb their jurisdiction, but they shall not even proceed against clerics or other ecclesiastical persons until the bishop has first been approached and has proved himself negligent in the matter; otherwise their proceedings and decisions avail nothing and they shall be bound to make satisfaction to the parties for the damage sustained. Moreover, if anyone should appeal in cases permitted by the law, or make a complaint regarding some grievance, or otherwise by reason of the lapse of two years, as was said above, have recourse to another judge, he shall be bound to transfer at his own expense to the judge of appeal all the acts of the proceedings conducted in the presence of the bishop, having previously, however, notified the bishop, so that if anything appears suitable to him for the direction of the cause, he may communicate it to the judge of appeal. But if the appellee appears, he shall also be bound to bear his proportion of the expenses of transferring the acts if he wishes to use them, unless it is a local custom to act otherwise, namely, that the entire costs are borne by the appellant. Furthermore, the notary shall be bound on receipt of a suitable fee to furnish the appellant as soon as possible and within at least one month with a copy of the proceedings, and should he through delay in supplying such copy be guilty of fraud, he shall at the discretion of the ordinary be suspended from the administration of his office and shall be compelled to pay double the costs of the suit, which is to be divided between the appellant and the poor of the locality. But if the judge himself should be aware of this delay, or should participate therein, or should in any other way hinder the delivery of the entire proceedings to the appellant within the time specified above, he shall be bound to the same penalty of paying double the costs, as was stated above; any privileges, indults, agreements which bind only their authors, and any other customs whatsoever to the contrary in respect to all matters dealt with above, notwithstanding.

APPENDIX

An earlier version of this brief study of St. Ignatius Loyola appeared in *Church History*, the journal of the American Society of Church History, 48, No. 4 (December 1979), 387–97. Because of its bearing on the theme I have developed here, I would like to call attention to an article by John W. O'Malley, s.j., in *Studies in the Spirituality of Jesuits*, 16, No. 2 (March 1984), 1–20: "To Travel to Any Part of the World: Jerónimo Nadal and the Jesuit Vocation."

The Idea of Pilgrimage in the Experience of Ignatius Loyola

THE IDEA OF PILGRIMAGE occupies an important place in the life and thought of Ignatius Loyola. In the autobiography that he dictated to a colleague late in his life he refers to himself throughout as "the pilgrim."[1] He actually went on a pilgrimage to Jerusalem, and describes in detail his long and difficult journey. His biographers too often use the term and imagery of pilgrimage when they write about his early years, yet the notion of pilgrimage in his life has never been explored to any extent; nor has its significance, I believe, been sufficiently taken into account.[2] In this essay I should like to focus on this theme and indicate what I consider to be its role and importance in his religious experience.

The term pilgrimage can be used in different senses.[3] The literal meaning, a journey to a shrine or sacred place as an act of religious devotion, describes a very old and common religious practice, one that has been part of Christian devotion since early times. As might be expected, Jerusalem, the city where Christ died and was buried, and other places in Judea associated with the life of Christ, were and have remained the chosen sites of Christian pilgrimage. Tombs of the saints and shrines of the Virgin Mary have also drawn the faithful over the course of the centuries. Rome, Compostela, Canterbury, Lourdes, and numerous other places have been and continue to be great pilgrimage centers.

The term can also be given an allegorical meaning. Life can be viewed as a pilgrimage, that is, as a journey fraught with obstacles and difficulties through this world to the world beyond. This notion of *homo viator*, man the wayfarer, also has old and established credentials in Christian thought. A classic statement of it appears in the Epistle to the Hebrews where the author speaks of those who had faith as "strangers or passing travelers on earth" and "longing for a better country—I mean, the heavenly one" (Hebr. 11:13–16, 13:14).[4] St. Augustine carried this concept into his *De civitate Dei* and frequently refers to the City of God as a stranger or pilgrim on this earth.[5] Many of the early Fathers saw the travels of Ulysses as symbolic of the voyage of the Christian soul through life, an allegory foreshadowing the dangerous journey of Christian in John Bunyan's *Pilgrim's Progress*.[6] Dante's journey in the *Divine Comedy* represents the journey that every man must make from the Dark Wood to the Eternal Light. Indeed, an actual or literal pilgrimage may be a kind of allegorical expression of life as a journey.

In addition to these meanings of the term, there is a third way of understanding the idea of pilgrimage: the spiritual sense or the extended notion of the term. A pilgrimage can be a search, that is, an essentially interior journey toward some goal or ideal. It can involve the pursuit of meaning or a mission for one's life, and it may effect inward growth or transformation. Léon Bloy was called "the pilgrim of the Absolute" in this sense, and long before that St. Bonaventure wrote a treatise known as *Itinerarium* wherein he describes the stages of the mind's journey to God. In these instances the term refers essentially to an interior movement or progress, and it signifies, I think, a sublimation or spiritualization of the literal notion of pilgrimage. When St. Bernard of Clairvaux told his monks that "your cell is Jerusalem," he was recommending this kind of inward or spiritual journey. By the same token the external pilgrimage to a sacred place may symbolize or in some way reflect man's inward search.

The various meanings of pilgrimage tend to merge at the deeper level. The reason perhaps is that they are all rooted in the concept of man the traveler, the person en route toward some destination, toward some end. This perspective seems to lie deep in the human consciousness and to have significance far beyond that of mere physical travel. In his book entitled *Homo Viator*, the French philosopher Gabriel Marcel gives one explanation. He sees our human values as having meaning and validity only in relation to an order beyond this world, a higher or greater reality toward which man himself is journeying.[7] He says:

Perhaps a stable order can only be established if man is acutely
aware of his condition as a traveller, that is to say, if he perpetually
reminds himself that he is required to cut himself a dangerous path
across the unsteady blocks of a universe which has collapsed and
seems to be crumbling in every direction. This path leads to a
world more firmly established in Being, a world whose changing
and uncertain gleams are all that we can discern here below. Does
not everything happen as though this ruined universe turned relent-
lessly upon whoever claimed that he could settle down in it. . . .[8]

There may be other theories about the origin of this archetypal
idea which seems to be universal, but the quotation from Marcel
aptly serves to bring us back to Ignatius Loyola. To judge from his
autobiography, he was a man "acutely aware of his condition as a
traveller." This awareness had its origins in his conversion and in
the pilgrimage he undertook to the Holy Land, but Ignatius'
continuing reference to himself as "the pilgrim" throughout his
story and his use of the term itself after so many years had gone
by suggest a meaning beyond the purely literal one. What is the
nature of his pilgrimage, his pilgrim status? How does the concept
develop or his understanding change in the course of his active
life?

These are not questions usually raised in connection with Ignatius Loyola. As founder of the Jesuits, as author of the *Spiritual
Exercises*, as one of the outstanding figures of the Counter-Reformation, he is more commonly discussed in terms of the soldier,
as the man who even as a religious leader or spiritual guide
thought and planned along military lines. Despite the crude
stereotype, the "soldier of Christ" metaphor is an ancient and
venerable one, and Ignatius, like Erasmus and others in his day,
made significant use of it. It was probably congenial to him, for
he had been a soldier before his conversion in 1521, but its
importance should not be exaggerated. It is not the key to Ignatius
and the Society of Jesus. Indeed, there are other, more profound
facets of his thought. And there is, as indicated, the image of the
pilgrim upon which this study will focus. It will have the merit at
least of approaching Ignatius from a different angle and of consid-
ering his experience in different terms.

Ignatius was a Spanish *caballero*, an *hidalgo* not entirely unlike the fictional Don Quixote. He was born in the Basque province of Guipuzcoa in the old Kingdom of Castile in 1491. The site of his family's property and castle was Loyola, and he was originally known as Iñigo López de Loyola. Ignatius was a name he adopted many years later out of devotion to the early church Father St. Ignatius of Antioch. In his youth he was put into the household of the royal treasurer of Spain, Juan Valezquez de Cuellar, where he had a generous introduction to courtly life. In 1517 he entered the service of the Duke of Najera, the Spanish viceroy of Navarre. Spain had recently conquered and annexed that province along the Pyrenees, and the danger that France would intervene to restore the former ruling house was realized in the spring of 1521. The French army crossed the Pyrenees and advanced into Navarre; they took the capital, Pamplona, and laid seige to its citadel. Ignatius, among the defenders, was seriously wounded during the French bombardment by a cannon ball that shattered one leg and badly damaged the other. He was taken to Loyola to recover from his wounds, and in the months of convalescence that followed, Ignatius underwent a profound change of heart. He gave up all thoughts of worldly fame and fortune and decided to follow the path of the saints and do great deeds for the love of God.

This conversion was inspired by two religious works that he read at Loyola, a life of Christ and a collection of saints' lives known as *Flos sanctorum*, in lieu of the novels of chivalry he would have preferred.[9] As he read and pondered these tomes during his convalescence, he asked himself, as told in his autobiography. " 'What if I should do what St. Francis did, what St. Dominic did?' " and he thought "of going to Jerusalem, barefoot and eating nothing but herbs and undergoing all the other rigors that he saw the saints had endured" (A 23–24). Indeed, his whole attention now centered on going to the Holy Land as a penitent pilgrim as soon as he was able. Ignatius' conversion from the very start was thus linked to the idea of a Jerusalem pilgrimage.

He set out on his journey in early 1522 and went first to the shrine of Our Lady of Montserrat in Catalonia, then to the nearby town of Manresa, where he remained for a year. Though an interruption of the Jerusalem trip, his experiences at Manresa were of the utmost importance in his spiritual development. He informs us that God instructed him like a schoolmaster, that his mind was enlightened, and his understanding immeasurably deepened (A 37–40). Specifically, he gained a clearer picture of what he should do in the service of Christ and a keener sense of an apostolate or mission. The pilgrimage to Jerusalem was not abandoned, but given a new purpose and a new dimension. He would stay in Jerusalem "continually visiting the holy places"; and "he also planned to help souls" (A 49).[10] A lifelong apostolate, the enterprise of converting the Moslems in the Holy Land, was added to the idea of his pilgrimage.

Ignatius had an eventful journey to Jerusalem. Sailing out of Barcelona without a penny, he first went to Rome where he received the blessing of the new pope, Adrian VI. He then traveled on to Venice, the port of embarkation for the East. It was a difficult time for pilgrims traveling to Jerusalem because of the militancy of the Ottoman Turks, but through the intervention of the Doge of Venice, Ignatius was given passage on a ship sailing to Cyprus, and from there he crossed over to the Holy Land. Needless to say, he was most impressed, recalling in particular a second visit to the Mount of Olives to see a stone that was believed to bear the footprints of Christ from the time of His Ascension (A 50–51). Though he firmly intended to stay, the Franciscan provincial who was in charge of the Christian holy places (the region was under Turkish rule) forbade Ignatius to remain and so most reluctantly he returned to Cyprus and, after a stormy trip, to Venice. Frustrated in his plan to stay in the East he debated what course he should now follow. Here is how he expresses the problem in the autobiography: "After the pilgrim realized that it was not God's will that he remain in Jerusalem, he continually pondered within himself what he ought to do. At last he inclined more to study for some time so he would be able to help souls, and he decided to go to Barcelona" (A 54).

What now follows is a period of more than ten years during which Ignatius pursued a formal education. He began with Latin instruction in Barcelona, went on to the University of Alcalá and then to Salamanca, and finally in 1528 to the University of Paris. He received his Master of Arts in Paris in 1534 and also studied theology with the Dominicans on the rue Saint-Jacques. Ignatius was never a great scholar or intellectual, but he did receive an extensive education, and was exposed to the intellectual and

religious currents then stirring Europe. The exceptional turmoil—
religious revolt, political conflict, overseas discovery and expansion—which could not have escaped Ignatius makes his subsequent
intention all the more interesting and unexpected.

While he was in Paris, Ignatius met and fostered the friendship
of several close companions. Their association or comradeship in
the spiritual life is what led eventually to the formation of the
Society of Jesus. For the time being, however, they were bound
together simply by a common religious ideal. They all proposed
to go to the Holy Land and labor for the conversion of the
Moslems, "to spend their lives," as Ignatius expresses it, "in the
service of souls" (A 80). On August 15, 1534, the feast of the
Assumption, Ignatius and six friends made vows to this effect in a
chapel on Montmartre. If they found it impossible to get to
Jerusalem or if they were not allowed to remain there after they
arrived, they agreed that they would go to Rome to offer their
services to the pope (A 80–81). Their prime intention, however,
was to go as pilgrims to the East, as pilgrims who would stay and
preach the Gospel of Christ where He Himself once lived and
preached. Ignatius' own aim of a Jerusalem apostolate had now
become a group plan, a "communitarian ideal."[11]

In 1535 Ignatius revisited Spain and then went to Venice where
nine companions from Paris joined him in early 1537. They
awaited a ship to the East, but none sailed, and the outbreak of
war between Venice and the Turks in mid-1537 made the prospect
unlikely. Late that year they set out for Rome and carried out the
alternative they had agreed on in Paris: they put themselves at the
disposition of Pope Paul III. The pope, it appears, urged them to
give up any thought of a Jerusalem apostolate and to remain in
Italy serving the church there. One of the companions, Nicholas
Bobadilla, reports that Paul told them "Italy is a good and true
Jerusalem," a remark very similar to that of St. Bernard to his
monks, and that this led to discussions among them of forming a
religious order.[12] These discussions were held in the spring of
1539, and in them the aims and outline of the Society of Jesus
were first formulated and set down.[13] The Jesuits thus came into
being as the substitution for the actual pilgrimage to Jerusalem
Ignatius and his friends had intended to make. The Grand Turk in

league with the pope, so to speak, had effected this historic change.

A very interesting transformation had occurred since the days of Ignatius' conversion back in 1521. His original notion of a chivalrous pilgrimage to the East had evolved into a religious order. The process took eighteen years, the key years of development that Ignatius covers in his autobiography. By his own designation they are his pilgrim years. The term can be understood in almost every sense of the word, literally, figuratively, psychologically, spiritually, but the story begins with the most literal and conventional meaning: the undertaking of an actual journey to Jerusalem. Why then did it develop the way it did? Along with this question are two other very closely related ones. What is the deeper significance of pilgrimage in the thought of Ignatius Loyola? To what extent did the new order, the Society of Jesus, reflect or embody the notion of pilgrimage? The answers to these questions carry us to the heart of Ignatius' vision.

Why did Ignatius' pilgrimage follow the course I have described? The explanation, I believe, lies in his experience at Manresa when he stopped for almost a year en route to Jerusalem. There, according to his own testimony, an enormous enlightment took place: he gained a new and better understanding of his spiritual purpose. This has always been associated with the two most important parts of the famous handbook or guide he composed known as the *Spiritual Exercises*, namely, the meditation on the Kingdom of Christ and the meditation on the Two Standards.[14] The first meditation centers on Christ as a king calling everyone to follow Him and to join His enterprise of winning over the whole world. In the second meditation, the theme is the choice confronting men of serving under the standard of the true commander, Christ, or under the standard of the rebel chief, Satan. These images derive from his convalescent reading at Loyola, but they became clearer and sharper at Manresa and were made the foundation of his religious vision and life's aim.

Ignatius asks throughout the *Spiritual Exercises* that one visualize the scenes he evokes; his expression is "to form a mental representation of the place." This means to place oneself imaginatively in the land where Christ was born, lived, and died, and to picture the scenes and places associated with His life. "Here it will be to see in imagination the synagogues, villages, and towns where Christ our Lord preached," he declares at the beginning of the meditation on the Kingdom of Christ. In the meditation on the Two Standards his instruction is to visualize a great plain about Jerusalem on the one hand and a vast plain about Babylon on the other where the two rival commanders are gathering and dispatching their forces. Here are the key points of his meditation on the Standard of Christ:

> Consider Christ our Lord, standing in a lowly place in a great plain about the region of Jerusalem, His appearance beautiful and attractive.
>
> Consider how the Lord of all the world chooses so many persons, apostles, disciples, etc., and sends them throughout the whole world to spread His sacred doctrine among all men, no matter what their state or condition.
>
> Consider the address which Christ our Lord makes to His servants and friends whom He sends on this enterprise, recommending to them to seek to help all. . . .[15]

There are a few conclusions I should like to draw from the substance and form of these meditations and from the *Spiritual Exercises* as a whole. The first is that Jerusalem is not simply the center or terminus of a pilgrimage but the place where Christ summons His followers, where He enlists them in His great enterprise, and from whence He dispatches them throughout the world. Ignatius' sense of mission or apostolate thus became closely bound up with his journey to Jerusalem, and Jerusalem itself became the logical place to go to join Christ and enter His service. The pilgrim journey now led to a new commitment and a new life of activity and apostolic service. Ignatius subsequently communicated this larger concept of pilgrimage to his friends in Paris, and it explains their vows on Montmartre and their desire to go to the East.

The second conclusion I would draw is that to Ignatius prayer is a type of pilgrimage. The *Spiritual Exercises* consists in large part of meditations on the life of Christ in which the exercitant is instructed always to envision the place mentally and to apply the senses to the scene: these are prayers based on a mental journey to the Holy Land. The exercitant visualizes the road from Nazareth to Bethlehem, observes the cave where Christ was born, sees the room of the Last Supper, pictures the great plain about Jerusalem where Christ is summoning His friends. The sacred scenes come alive in the imagination, and one is "as though present" in the holy places.[16] This down-to-earth realism in prayer, this emphasis on sense perception and experience, is one of the most characteristic and powerful aspects of Ignatian spirituality and reflects Ignatius' awareness of God's immanence in creation and of the human context and historical reality of the Christian mysteries. So also does his idea of pilgrimage to the East. Whether actually in the flesh or imaginatively in prayer he sought to know Christ in His human surroundings.

But we are now dealing with the deeper significance of pilgrimage in the thought of Ignatius without fully answering the first question posed: Why did Ignatius and his friends finally abandon their Jerusalem project and go to Rome? Unquestionably, the Turks blocked the way. In case of such an eventuality they had agreed to go to Rome to offer their services to the pope. What was the logic or justification of this alternate proposal? They saw the pope as "the vicar of Christ" and his direction as comparable to service under the Standard of Christ (A 80–81).[17] One of Ignatius' companions, Pierre Favre, in a letter written from Rome in November 1538, explained their decision by saying that the pope was "the lord of the entire harvest of Christ" and that he had "a greater knowledge of what is advantageous to the whole of Christendom."[18] They had preferred Jerusalem and an apostolate there, but Rome could be a second Jerusalem and from that center they could also go forth to spread Christ's doctrine throughout the world. This they now undertook to do as a Society designated by the name of Jesus under the auspices and direction of His vicar on earth. There is a consistent theme or thread, it seems to me, that runs from the original intention of Ignatius in 1521 to the formation of the Jesuits in 1539—the expanding concept of the Jerusalem pilgrimage.

I have touched on the deeper meaning of pilgrimage in the thought and spirituality of Ignatius, but there is an episode in his life that may serve to underscore the importance of the actual Holy Land in his devotion. He intended to say his first Mass there and waited for some time in order to do so.[19] He had been ordained a priest in Venice in June 1537, and according to his autobiography he decided to wait a year before saying Mass (A 89). This would coincide with the period during which all the companions were planning to wait for a ship to the East. Because of war between Venice and the Turks, they came to Rome in early 1538, but Ignatius continue to wait, it would seem, until he was certain the Jerusalem project could not be carried out and the pope had accepted their offer of service. He said his first Mass in Rome on Christmas day 1538, a year and a half after his ordination—an unusually long delay—and he chose the chapel of the Manger in the church of Santa Maria Maggiore as the place to celebrate it. This chapel was a very old replica of the grotto of the Nativity in Bethlehem, and it seems a fair assumption that it was a substitute for the actual site of Christ's birth where he had hoped to celebrate it. Ignatius' biographer Father Brodrick concludes his book *St. Ignatius Loyola: The Pilgrim Years* with a reference to this first Mass. "It marked in a sense," he tells us, "the renunciation of a long-cherished dream and the recognition that the *amor y servicio* of God our Lord required him to make Rome his Jerusalem."[20]

Rome indeed it was. Within the next few months the Society of Jesus came into being. Ignatius remained in the city for the rest of his days; his travels, his search, his pilgrimage in a sense had ended. He now presided over the far-flung activities of a growing and dynamic order whose members were the chief agents of Catholic revival in the sixteenth century. It was also an association of remarkable and outstanding personalities; their enterprises and achievements both in Europe and overseas are most impressive. Without entering into the history of the early Jesuits, I should like to consider the final question raised a short time back: To what extent did the new order reflect or embody the notion of pilgrimage?

The key to an answer lies in those two meditations in the *Spiritual Exercises* discussed earlier: the meditation on the Kingdom of Christ and the meditation on the Two Standards. The whole concept of a Holy Land pilgrimage–apostolate which these meditations expressed was now transposed and actualized in the form of active service under the pope at Rome. Under the new circumstances Ignatius and his companions in 1539 organized more formally as a religious order. Rome thus became their Jerusalem, and the papal banner the equivalent of the Standard of Christ. The statement of purpose and outline for the Society which they drew up is interesting to examine in this light.[21] Obedience to the pope as the vicar of Christ is one of its main features. In fact, the companions took a special vow to obey the pope, declaring that "whatever His Holiness commands pertaining to the advancement of souls and the propagation of the faith we must immediately carry out, without any evasion or excuse, as far as in us lies, whether he sends us to the Turks or to the New World or to the Lutherans or to others be they infidel or faithful" (A 107). It is not only the vow per se that is significant here, but also the going forth throughout the world at the pope's behest. This commitment is close indeed to the mediation on the Standard of Christ. And it is obvious that the travels of the companions were intended to continue. They were to remain essentially pilgrim priests.

In the more detailed Constitutions for the Society which Ignatius drafted in later years the stress on going forth into all parts of the world is retained. Explaining the special vow of obedience to the pope, Ignatius wrote: "This is a vow to go anywhere His Holiness will order, whether among the faithful or the infidels, without pleading an excuse and without requesting any expenses for the journey, for the sake of matters pertaining to the worship of God and the welfare of the Christian religion."[22] This same mobility is also prescribed in other parts of the Constituions: the Jesuits "should always be ready to travel about in various regions of the world" (C 104). Indeed, Ignatius declared that "our vocation is to travel through the world and to live in any part of it whatsoever where there is hope of greater service to God and of help of souls" (C 170; see also 172, 267). A colleague and companion of Ignatius' from Paris, Francis Xavier, has given us the classic example of this basic vocational aim. Gabriel Marcel's *homo viator* has no truer embodiment.

In another way, too, the Constitutions of the Society reflect a concern with pilgrimage. In the training of candidates who seek to join the new order, Ignatius specified "six principal testing experiences," one of which was to make a pilgrimage. "The third experience is to spend another month in making a pilgrimage

without money and even in begging from door to door, at
appropriate times, for the love of God our Lord, in order to grow
accustomed to discomfort in food and lodging. Thus too the
candidate, through abandoning all the reliance which he could
have in money or other created things, may with genuine faith
and intense love place his reliance entirely in his Creator and
Lord" (C 97). Clearly, the test derives from Ignatius' own early
experience as a pilgrim and is, as Joseph de Guibert calls it, "an
exercise in humility and abnegation," but it is also a training and
a preparation for the later journeys the members of the Society
will be called upon to undertake.[23]

I have indicated what I consider to be the character and significance of Ignatius' idea of pilgrimage. It had begun as a desire to
do something notable for the love of God and ended as a dynamic
and effective religious order. The notion of pilgrimage encom-
passes this development from beginning to end as the thrust was
continually and literally toward Jerusalem, toward the historic and
sacred center, and toward the following and serving of Christ in
the human context. That is the meaning, as I understand it, of
Ignatius' continual reference to himself in the autobiography as
"the pilgrim." It is true that Rome at length replaced Jerusalem,
but the thrust remained the same, and the transposition of centers
was not that important for one who had reached the psychological
and theological perspective of Ignatius. "In Christ our Lord, the
bridegroom, and in His spouse the Church, only one Spirit holds
sway," he wrote in the "Rules for Thinking with the Church"
which he appended to the *Spiritual Exercises*. And that same Spirit,
he believed, would guide and inspire him as he labored in Rome.

NOTES

1. *The Autobiography of St. Ignatius Loyola*, ed. Olin. Subsequent
references to this volume will be indicated by the letter A and will, with
one exception, be included within parentheses in the text.

2. The Jesuit historian James Brodrick entitled his study of Ignatius'
early years *Saint Ignatius Loyola: The Pilgrim Years, 1491–1538* (New York:
Farrar, Straus and Cudahy, 1956); and Macdonald Hastings gives the
caption "Pilgrimage" to the middle and main portions of his memoir

Jesuit Child (New York: St. Martin's, 1971), in which he recounts the story of Ignatius and the Jesuits. The Spanish Ignatian scholar Pedro de Leturia, s.j., however, is the only author I know who has specifically discussed the pilgrimage theme. See his "Jerusalén y Roma en los designios de San Ignacio de Loyola," *Estudios ignacianos.* I. *Estudios biográficos,* rev. Ignacio Iparraguirre, s.j. (Rome: Institutum Historicum S. I., 1957), pp. 181–200. Javier Osuna, s.j., *Friends in the Lord,* trans. Nicholas King, s.j. (London: The Way, 1974), is a penetrating study of Ignatius' experience and the origins of the Society of Jesus and emphasizes throughout the notion of pilgrimage.

3. There is much relevant material on this topic. Here are a few references that may be helpful and suggestive: Ekkart Sauser, "Pilgrimage," in *Sacramentum Mundi: An Encyclopedia of Theology,* edd. Karl Rahner et al., 6 vols. (New York: Herder and Herder, 1968–1970), v 26–28; Eberhart Simons, "Sacred Times and Place," in ibid., 387–88; Léon-E. Halkin, "Erasme Pélerin," in *Scrinium Erasmianum,* ed. Joseph Coppens, 2 vols. (Leiden: Brill, 1969), ii, 239–52; Gerhart B. Ladner, "*Homo Viator*: Medieval Ideas on Alienation and Order," *Speculum,* 42, No. 2 (1967), 233–59; and Thomas Berry, "Contemporary Spirituality: The Journey of the Human Community," *Cross Currents,* 24, Nos. 2–3 (Summer/Fall 1974), 172–83. I might note too the currency of notions of the evolutionary or biological journey of life through the eons, as in Loren Eiseley, *The Immense Journey* (New York: Time Books, 1962) and in the writings of the Jesuit paleontologist Teilhard de Chardin.

4. A memorable passage in the correspondence of Erasmus echoes this basic Christian concept. In a letter of September 1522 refusing Zwingli's offer of citizenship in Zurich, Erasmus wrote: "I wish to be a citizen of the world, belonging everywhere, or perhaps better a pilgrim. Would that I might be enrolled in the heavenly city! For I aim toward it, though so many ailments repeatedly recur." Ep. 1314, *Opus epistolarum,* edd. Allen, Allen, and Garrod, v 129.

5. *The City of God,* trans. Marcus Dods (New York: Modern Library, 1950), pp. 3, 483–84, 668.

6. Hugo Rahner, s.j., *Greek Myths and Christian Mystery,* trans. Brian Battershaw (New York: Harper & Row, 1963), pp. xx, 328–30.

7. Trans. Emma Craufurd (Chicago: Regnery, 1951), especially "Preface" and "Value and Immortality."

8. Ibid., pp. 153–54.

9. Pedro de Leturia, s.j., *Iñigo de Loyola,* trans. Aloysius J. Owen, s.j. (Syracuse: Le Moyne College Press, 1949), pp. 83–85.

10. See also Hugo Rahner, s.j., *The Spirituality of St. Ignatius Loyola: An Account of Its Historical Development,* trans. Francis John Smith (Westminster, Md.: Newman, 1953), p. 57, and Osuna, *Friends,* p. 27.

11. Osuna, *Friends*, pp. 18–20, 52–58. Juan de Polanco, Ignatius' secretary later in Rome, states: " 'The first companions whom our Father Ignatius gathered at Paris, and he himself, did not go to Italy to found an order, but to go to Jerusalem and to preach and die amongst the infidel.' " Quoted in Paul Dudon, s.j., *St. Ignatius of Loyola*, trans. William J. Young, s.j. (Milwaukee: Bruce, 1949), p. 235*n*15.

12. Osuna, *Friends*, pp. 90–91, and Leturia, "Jerusalén y Roma," 198–99, and idem, "Importancia de año 1538 en el cumplimiento del 'Voto de Montmartre,' " *Estudios ignacianos*. I. *Estudios biográficos*, rev. Ignacio Iparraguirre, s.j. (Rome: Institutum Historicum S. I., 1957), pp. 215–16.

13. See the First Sketch (or *Formula instituti*) in the document section above.

14. Osuna, *Friends*, pp. 12–20, and Rahner, *Spirituality of Ignatius*, pp. 34–36. The two meditations will be found in *Spiritual Exercises*, ed. Puhl, pp. 43–45 and 61–63.

15. *Spiritual Exercises*, ed. Puhl, pp. 61–62.

16. Ibid., p. 52. On "the application of the senses," see Hugo Rahner, s.j., *Ignatius the Theologian*, trans. Michael Barry (New York: Herder and Herder, 1968), chap. 5.

17. See note 13 above.

18. See this letter in the document section above.

19. See Pedro de Leturia, s.j., "La primera misa de San Ignacio de Loyola y sus relaciones con la fundación de la Compañía," *Estudios ignacianos*. I. *Estudios biográficos*, rev. Ignacio Iparraguirre, s.j. (Rome: Institutum Historicum S. I., 1957), pp. 223–35.

20. P. 257.

21. See note 13 above.

22. The *Constitutions of the Society of Jesus*, trans. George E. Ganss, s.j. (St. Louis: The Institute of Jesuit Sources, 1970), pp. 79–80. Further references to this text will be indicated by the letter C and included within parentheses in the text.

23. *The Jesuits: Their Spiritual Doctrine and Practice*, trans. William J. Young, s.j. (Chicago: Loyola University Press, 1964), pp. 103–104.

BIBLIOGRAPHY OF WORKS CITED

Alberigo, Giuseppe. "La 'reception' du Concile de Trente par l'Eglise catholique romaine." *Irénikon*, 58 (1985), 311–37.

Annales Camaldulenses. Edd. J. B. Mittarelli and A. Costadoni. 9 vols. Venice, 1755–1773.

Augustine. *The City of God.* Trans. Marcus Dods. New York: Modern Library, 1950.

Bangert, William V., s.j. *A History of the Society of Jesus.* St. Louis: The Institute of Jesuit Sources, 1972.

Bataillon, Marcel. *Erasme et l'Espagne: Recherches sur l'histoire spirituelle du xvie siècle.* Paris: Droz, 1937.

Bentley, Jerry H. *Humanists and Holy Writ.* Princeton: Princeton University Press, 1983.

Berry, Thomas. "Contemporary Spirituality: The Journey of the Human Community." *Cross Currents*, 24, Nos. 2–3 (Summer/Fall 1974), 172–83.

Bossy, John. *Christianity in the West, 1400–1700.* Oxford: Oxford University Press, 1985.

Brodrick, James, s.j. *Saint Ignatius Loyola: The Pilgrim Years, 1491–1538.* New York: Farrar, Straus and Cudahy, 1956.

Canons and Decrees of the Council of Trent. Trans. H. J. Schroeder, o.p. St. Louis: B. Herder, 1941.

Cesareo, Francesco C. *Humanism and Catholic Reform: The Life and Work of Gregorio Cortese, 1483–1548.* Bern: Lang, 1990.

Christian Humanism and the Reformation: Selected Writings of Erasmus. Ed. John C. Olin. 3rd ed. New York: Fordham University Press, 1987.

Cochrane, Eric. *Italy, 1530–1630.* Ed. Julius Kirshner. London and New York: Longmans, 1988.

Concilium Tridentinum: Diariorum, actorum, epistolarum, tractatuum nova collectio. Edd. S. Merkle et al. 13 vols. Freiburg: Görresgesellschaft, 1901–1938.

Delumeau, Jean. *Catholicism Between Luther and Voltaire: A New View of the Counter-Reformation*. London: Burns & Oates; Philadelphia: Westminster, 1977.

———. *Le Christianisme va-t-il mourir?* Paris: Hachette, 1978.

Dickens, A. G. *The Counter Reformation*. New York: Harcourt, Brace & World, 1969.

Dudon, Paul, s.j. *St. Ignatius of Loyola*. Trans. William J. Young, s.j. Milwaukee: Bruce, 1949.

Duggan, Lawrence G. "The Unresponsiveness of the Late Medieval Church: A Reconsideration." *The Sixteenth Century Journal*, 9, No. 1 (April 1978), 3–26.

Eiseley, Loren. *The Immense Journey*. New York: Time Books, 1962.

Endean, Philip, s.j. "Who Do You Say Ignatius Is? Jesuit Fundamentalism and Beyond." *Studies in the Spirituality of Jesuits*, 19, No. 5 (November 1987), 1–53.

Erasmus, Desiderius. *The Colloquies of Erasmus*. Trans. Craig R. Thompson. Chicago: The University of Chicago Press, 1965.

———. *The Correspondence of Erasmus* I. Trans. R. A. B. Mynors. Toronto: University of Toronto Press, 1974.

———. *Opus epistolarum Des. Erasmi Roterodami*. Edd. P. S. Allen, H. M. Allen, and H. W. Garrod. 12 vols. Oxford: Clarendon, 1906–1958.

Evennett, H. Outram. "The New Orders." In *The New Cambridge Modern History*. II. *The Reformation, 1520–1559*. Ed. G. R. Elton. Cambridge: Cambridge University Press, 1962.

———. *The Spirit of the Counter-Reformation*. Ed. John Bossy. Cambridge: Cambridge University Press, 1968.

Febvre, Lucien. *A New Kind of History*. Ed. Peter Burke. London: Routledge & Kegan Paul, 1973.

———. "Une question mal posée: Les origines de la réforme française et le problème de la réforme." *Au coeur religieux du xvie siècle*. Paris: Sevpen, 1957.

Fenlon, Dermot. "*Encore une question*: Lucien Febvre, the Reformation, and the School of *Annales*." *Historical Studies*, 9 (1956), 65–81.

———. *Heresy and Obedience in Tridentine Italy: Cardinal Pole and the Counter Reformation*. Cambridge: Cambridge University Press, 1972.

Gilbert, Felix. "Religion and Politics in the Thought of Gasparo Contarini." In *Action and Conviction in Early Modern Europe*. Edd. Theodore K. Rabb and Jerrold E. Seigel. Princeton: Princeton University Press, 1969. Pp. 90–116.

Green, Otis H. *Spain and the Western Tradition* III. Madison: University of Wisconsin Press, 1965.

Guibert, Joseph de, s.j. *The Jesuits: Their Spiritual Doctrine and Practice*. Trans. William J. Young, s.j. Chicago: Loyola University Press, 1964.

Halkin, Léon-E. "Erasme Pélerin." In *Scrinium Erasmianum*. Ed. Joseph Coppens. 2 vols. Leiden: Brill, 1969. II 239–52.

Hall, Basil. "The Trilingual College of San Ildefonso and the Making of the Complutensian Polyglot Bible." In *Studies in Church History*. v. *The Church and Academic Learning*. Ed. G. J. Cuming. Leiden: Brill, 1969. Pp. 114–46.

Hallmann, Barbara McClung. *Italian Cardinals, Reform, and the Church as Property*. Berkeley: University of California Press, 1985.

Hastings, Macdonald. *Jesuit Child*. New York: St. Martin's, 1971.

Hudon, William V. "Papal, Episcopal, and Secular Authority in the Work of Marcello Cervini." *Cristianesimo nella storia*, 9 (1988), 493–521.

Jedin, Hubert. *Crisis and Closure of the Council of Trent: A Retrospective View from the Second Vatican Council*. Trans. N. D. Smith. London: Sheed & Ward, 1967.

———. *A History of the Council of Trent* I–II. Trans. Dom Ernest Graf, O.S.B. St. Louis: B. Herder, 1957, 1961.

———. "Trent, Council of." In *The New Catholic Encyclopedia*. 18 vols. New York: McGraw-Hill, 1976. XIV 271–78.

Ladner, Gerhard B. "*Homo Viator*: Medieval Ideas on Alienation and Order." *Speculum*, 42, No. 2 (April 1967), 233–59.

Leturia, Pedro de, S.J. "Importancia del año 1538 en el cumplimiento del 'Voto de Montmartre.'" *Estudios ignacianos*. I. *Estudios biográficos*. Rev. Ignacio Iparraguirre, S.J. Rome: Institutum Historicum S. I., 1957. Pp. 201–21.

———. *Iñigo de Loyola*. Trans. Aloysius J. Owen, S.J. Syracuse: Le Moyne College Press, 1949.

———. "Jerusalén y Roma en los designios de San Ignacio de Loyola." *Estudios ignacianos*. I. *Estudios biográficos*. Rev. Ignacio Iparraguirre, S.J. Rome: Institutum Historicum S. I., 1957. Pp. 181–200.

———. "La primera misa de San Ignacio de Loyola y sus relaciones con la fundación de la Compañia." *Estudios ignacianos*. I. *Estudios biográficos*. Rev. Ignacio Iparraguirre, S.J. Rome: Institutum Historicum S. I., 1957. Pp. 233–35.

Loyola, Ignatius. *The Autobiography of St. Ignatius Loyola*. Ed. John C. Olin. Trans. Joseph F. O'Callaghan. New York: Harper & Row, 1974.

———. *The Constitutions of the Society of Jesus*. Trans. George E. Ganss, S.J. St. Louis: The Institute of Jesuit Sources, 1970.

———. *The Spiritual Exercises of St. Ignatius*. Ed. Louis J. Puhl, S.J. Westminster, Md.: Newman, 1951.

Lubac, Henri de, S.J. *Catholicism*. New York: Longmans, 1950.

———. *Exégèse médiévale*. Paris: Aubier, 1964. Second Part, II.

Luther, Martin. *Luther's Works*. Edd. Helmuth Lehmann, Jaroslav Pelikan, et al. 56 vols. St. Louis: Concordia, 1955–.

McNally, Robert E., s.j. "The Council of Trent and the German Protestants." *Theological Studies*, 25, No. 1 (March 1964), 1–22.

Mandrou. Robert. *From Humanism to Science, 1480–1700.* Trans. Brian Pearce. Harmondsworth: Penguin, 1978.

Mansi, G. D. *Sacrorum conciliorum nova et amplissima collectio.* 53 vols. in 58. Paris: Welter, 1901–1927.

Marcel, Gabriel. *Homo Viator.* Trans. Emma Craufurd. Chicago: Regnery, 1951.

Matheson, Peter. *Cardinal Contarini at Regensburg.* Oxford: Clarendon, 1972.

Maurenbrecher, Wilhelm. *Geschichte der katholischen Reformation.* Nordlingen: Beck, 1880.

Minnich, Nelson H., and Gleason, Elisabeth G. "Vocational Choices: An Unknown Letter of Pietro Querini to Gasparo Contarini and Niccolò Tiepolo (April, 1512)." *The Catholic Historical Review*, 75 (1989), 1–20.

Monti, G. M. *Ricerche su Papa Paolo IV Carafa* I. Benevento: Cooperativi Tipografi, 1923.

Monumenta Historica Societatis Iesu. Monumenta Ignatiana. I. Sancti Ignatii de Loyola, Societatis Iesu fundatoris, epistolae et instructiones. 11 vols. Madrid: López, 1903–1911.

Monumenta Historica Societatis Iesu. Monumenta Ignatiana. III. Sancti Ignatii de Loyola Constitutiones Societatis Iesu. 2 vols. Rome: Borgo Sancto Spirito V, 1934–1936.

Oakley, Francis. *The Western Church in the Later Middle Ages.* Ithaca: Cornell University Press, 1979.

Olin, John C. "The Catholic Reformation." In *The Meaning of the Renaissance and the Reformation.* Ed. Richard L. DeMolen. Boston: Houghton-Mifflin, 1974. Pp. 267–93.

———. *The Catholic Reformation: Savonarola to Ignatius Loyola.* New York: Harper & Row, 1969.

———. "Erasmus and St. Ignatius Loyola." *Six Essays on Erasmus.* New York: Fordham University Press, 1979. Pp. 75–92.

———. "The Idea of Pilgrimage in the Experience of Ignatius Loyola." *Church History*, 48, No. 4 (December 1979), 387–97.

———. *Six Essays on Erasmus.* New York: Fordham University Press, 1979.

O'Malley, John W., s.j. *Giles of Viterbo on Church and Reform.* Leiden: Brill, 1968.

———. "The Jesuits, St. Ignatius, and the Counter Reformation: Some Recent Studies and Their Implications for Today." *Studies in the Spirituality of Jesuits*, 14, No. 1 (January 1982), 1–28.

————. "To Travel to Any Part of the World: Jerónimo Nadal and the Jesuit Vocation." *Studies in the Spirituality of Jesuits*, 16, No. 2 (March 1984), 1–20.

Osuna, Javier, s.j. *Friends in the Lord*. Trans. Nicholas King, s.j. London: The Way, 1974.

Ozment, Steven. *The Age of Reform, 1250–1550*. New Haven: Yale University Press, 1980.

Pastor, Ludwig. *The History of the Popes from the Close of the Middle Ages*. Trans. F. I. Antrobus, R. F. Kerr, et al. 40 vols. St. Louis: B. Herder, 1891–1953.

Peters, Edward. *Inquisition*. New York: Free Press, 1988. Repr. Berkeley, University of California Press, 1989.

Prodi, Paolo. "The Application of the Tridentine Decrees: The Organization of the Diocese of Bologna During the Episcopate of Cardinal Gabriele Paleotti." In *The Late Italian Renaissance*. Ed. Eric Cochrane. New York: Harper & Row, 1970. Pp. 226–43.

Quinn, Peter A. "Ignatius Loyola and Gian Pietro Carafa: Catholic Reformers at Odds." *The Catholic Historical Review*, 67 (1981), 386–400.

Rahner, Hugo, s.j. *Greek Myths and Christian Mystery*. Trans. Brian Battershaw. New York: Harper & Row, 1963.

————. *Ignatius the Theologian*. Trans. Michael Barry. New York: Herder and Herder, 1968.

————. *The Spirituality of St. Ignatius Loyola: An Account of Its Historical Development*. Trans. Francis J. Smith. Westminster, Md.: Newman, 1953.

Reform Thought in Sixteenth-Century Italy. Ed. Elisabeth G. Gleason. Chico, Calif.: Scholars Press, 1981.

A Reformation Debate: Sadoleto's Letter to the Genevans and Calvin's Reply. Ed. John C. Olin. New York: Harper & Row, 1966.

Reinhard, Wolfgang. "Reformation, Counter-Reformation, and the Early Modern State: A Reassessment." *The Catholic Historical Review*, 75 (1989), 383–404.

Rice, Eugene F., Jr. *The Foundations of Early Modern Europe, 1460–1559*. New York: Norton, 1970.

————. "The Humanist Idea of Christian Antiquity: Lefèvre d'Etaples and His Circle." *Studies in the Renaissance*, 9 (1962), 126–41.

Ross, J. B. "Gasparo Contarini and His Friends.' *Studies in the Renaissance*, 17 (1970), 192–232.

Rupp, Ernest Gordon. *Luther's Progress to the Diet of Worms*. New York: Harper & Row, 1964.

Sauser, Ekkart. "Pilgrimage." In *Sacramentum Mundi: An Encyclopedia of*

Theology. Edd. Karl Rahner et al. 6 vols. New York: Herder and Herder, 1968–1970. v 26–28.

San Carlo Borromeo: Catholic Reform and Ecclesiastical Politics in the Second Half of the Sixteenth Century. Edd. John M. Headley and John B. Tomaro. Washington, D.C.: Folger Books, 1988.

Schenk, Wilhelm. *Reginald Pole, Cardinal of England*. London and New York: Longmans, 1950.

Simons, Eberhart. "Sacred Times and Places." In *Sacramentum Mundi: An Encyclopedia of Theology*. Edd. Karl Rahner et al. 6 vols. New York: Herder and Herder, 1968–1970. v 387–88.

Stinger, Charles. *Humanism and the Church Fathers*. Albany: State University of New York Press, 1977.

Tolnay, Charles de. *Michaelangelo. V. The Final Period*. Princeton: Princeton University Press, 1971.

Tomaro, John B. "San Carlo Borromeo and the Implementation of the Council of Trent." In *San Carlo Borromeo: Catholic Reform and Ecclesiastical Politics in the Second Half of the Sixteenth Century*. Edd. John M. Headley and John B. Tomaro. Washington, D.C.: Folger Books, 1988. Pp. 67–84.

Trevor-Roper, H. R. *Historical Essays*. New York: Harper & Row, 1966.

Trinkaus, Charles. *In Our Image and Likeness: Humanity and Divinity in Italian Humanist Thought*. 2 vols. Chicago: The University of Chicago Press, 1970.

INDEX NOMINUM